THE ECONOMIC SYSTEM OF ISLAM

THE ECONOMIC SYSTEM OF ISLAM
(An English rendering of Islām kā Iqtiṣādī Niẓām)

﷽

by
Ḥaḍrat Khalīfatul-Masīḥ II,
Mirza Bashir-ud-Din Mahmud Ahmad
(may Allah be pleased with him)

ISLAM INTERNATIONAL PUBLICATIONS
TILFORD, SURREY

The Economic System of Islam
An English rendering of: *Islām kā Iqtiṣādī Niẓām*

A speech delivered by:
Ḥaḍrat Mirza Bashir-ud-Din Mahmud Ahmad[ra],
Khalīfatul-Masīḥ II,
on February 26, 1945 at Ahmadiyya Hostel, Lahore, Pakistan.

First published in English in UK in 2013

© Islam International Publications Ltd.

Published by
Islam International Publications Ltd.
Islamabad, Sheephatch Lane
Tilford, Surrey GU10 2AQ

Printed at
Raqeem Press
Islamabad, Tilford, Surrey

For further information you may visit www.alislam.org.

ISBN 978-1-84880-089-2

CONTENTS

Foreword... *vii*

THE ECONOMIC SYSTEM OF ISLAM............. 1
Importance of the Subject... 1
Sovereignty of Allah and its Implications for Those in Authority.. 2
Types of Economic Systems in the World 15
Teachings of Islam for Establishing a Just Society 17
Measures to End the Institution of Slavery 28
Impact of Religion Upon the Economic Systems 35
The Islamic Economic System................................... 37
Barriers to Illegitimate Accumulation of Wealth in Islam.. 53
Measures Adopted in Shariah to Achieve a Just Economic System... 60
Responsibilities of the Government 65
Communism... 72
Objections Against Communism on the Basis of Religion... 74
Prospect of Russia Emerging as Global Economic Shock.. 107
A Proper Economic System 124

Responsibilities of Rich Towards Poor 125
Prophecies About Russia 126
Concluding Observations 138

Publishers' Note *141*
Glossary *145*
Index *149*

FOREWORD

We are pleased to publish a new translation of a lecture delivered by Ḥaḍrat Mirza Bashir-ud-Din Mahmud Ahmad[ra], second Successor of the Promised Messiah[as], entitled, *Islām kā Iqtiṣādī Niẓām* [*The Economic System of Islam*]. The lecture was delivered in Lahore, at the Ahmadiyya Hostel, on February 26, 1945. The main purpose of the lecture is to show that it is only through the teachings of Islam that a truly just system of governance and economic system can be established.

Drawing on the Holy Quran, the lecture spells out the responsibilities of both the rulers and the ruled, and leaves no doubt that the Islamic system of governance is fundamentally democratic, based on free and fair elections in the best sense of the word. It also ensures that justice will prevail, incentives for achieving excellence would be provided, and the basic needs of all will be satisfied. However, a proper governance structure is a pre-requisite for the establishment of the Islamic economic system—it would be impossible to have an Islamic economic system in an otherwise corrupt political and social environment.

After describing in depth the main elements of the Islamic system of economics, the second half of the lecture is devoted to a critical evaluation of communism. It is demonstrated that the communist system is really not what it claims to be, and it has inherent contradiction which will cause its downfall. This is followed by a presentation of three prophecies about the decline of the Communist system in Russia—a prophecy of Prophet Ḥizqīl[as] [Ezekiel], a prophecy of the Promised Messiah[as], and a dream of the author himself containing the prophecy. The events that have unfolded since the lecture was given in 1945 demonstrate a remarkable fulfilment of these prophecies.

Our thanks are due to all those friends who have contributed towards the current revised English translation of this lecture. An earlier translation of Mr. A. Q. Niaz had been published by *Wakālat-e-Tabshīr*. The present version is revised under the supervision of Additional *Wakālat-e-Taṣnīf* by Dr. Iftikhar Ahmad Ayaz OBE, Munawar Ahmed Saeed and Dr. Irfan ul Haque with assistance from Dr. Atif Mian and Ahmed Saeed. We are grateful for the valuable assistance provided by Naveed Malik, Kashif Baloch, and Rashida Rana. May Allah the Almighty reward them all.

It may be noted that headings given in this translation are from the publishers.

Munir-ud-Din Shams
Additional Wakīlut-Taṣnīf
London, August 2013

بِسْمِ اللَّهِ الرَّحْمٰنِ الرَّحِيْمِ
نَحْمَدُهُ وَ نُصَلِّىْ عَلٰى رَسُوْلِهِ الْكَرِيْمِ[1]

THE ECONOMIC SYSTEM OF ISLAM

After reciting *tashahhud*, *ta'awwudh* and *Sūrah al-Fātiḥah*, Ḥuḍūr[ra] said:

Importance of the Subject

My sermon today deals with the economic system of Islam. This is a vast subject that is hard to address thoroughly within the limited time available. Discussion can at times become ambiguous and its import difficult to grasp if, for the sake of brevity, the core elements and context of the subject are not properly explained. Nonetheless, I shall endeavour—as far as possible—to present a succinct account of the Islamic economic system in a way that is easy to understand,

---

[1] In the name of Allah, the Gracious, the Merciful. We praise Him and send blessings on His exalted Prophet[sa]. (publishers)

and to explain its fundamental principles and the broader environment in which they have been placed.

Since Islamic economic system has certain features that appear to be in common with the so-called Communist system, my discourse would be incomplete if I did not describe the Islamic viewpoint regarding Communism and did not elucidate the differences between the two economic systems.

It should be remembered that just as branches grow out of the stem of a tree, important issues sprout out of the established prior fundamentals. Without an understanding of these fundamentals, the significance of those issues cannot be fully appreciated. I therefore deem it necessary that, before describing the Islamic economic system, I should briefly explain the foundation on which it rests.

Sovereignty of Allah and its Implications for Those in Authority

Islam lays the foundation of all its systems, whether political, economic, social or any other, on one fundamental principle—that the ultimate sovereignty and ownership belongs only to God Almighty. As it is stated in *Sūrah az-Zukhruf* that:[2]

$$\text{تَبَارَكَ الَّذِي لَهُ مُلْكُ السَّمٰوٰتِ وَالْأَرْضِ وَمَا بَيْنَهُمَا ۚ وَعِنْدَهُ عِلْمُ السَّاعَةِ ۚ وَإِلَيْهِ تُرْجَعُونَ ۝}$$

---

[2] *Sūrah az-Zukhruf,* 43:86, (publishers)

That is, greatly blessed is Allah to whom belongs the kingdom of the heavens and the earth. Similarly, all that is between them is also under His ownership and control. To Him also belongs the knowledge of the last Hour—when all of these have served their purpose and the time for them to perish has arrived. Ultimately, everything will be brought back to Him.

In this verse Almighty God announces that the rules over the heavens and the earth and whatever lies between the two is under His ownership and control. Furthermore, it is God alone who knows the destined time when every living being, after fulfilling the purpose of its creation, must face its end and return to Almighty Allah. In brief, this verse lays down that the kingdom of the heavens and earth really belongs to God, and everything that exists therein is destined to return to Him.

When a person is made responsible for a specific task, or is entrusted with something of value, he is answerable to the one who entrusted him with those responsibilities; but a person who regards himself free and unanswerable to anyone would be inclined to do whatever he pleases. This verse of the Holy Quran is a reminder that all worldly governments, kingdoms and powers are under God's command and are granted to human beings only as a trust. Man must not consider himself unaccountable just because he has the power and ownership of material wealth that he is given in this world. He may appear to have authority and ownership on the surface, but in truth he is only holding a trust from God. Human beings are answerable before God that they rightfully discharged the trust that was reposed in them.

Authority Emanates from Allah

The Holy Quran categorically declares that authority emanates from God and no individual has any inherent right over it. It is stated:[3]

$$\text{قُلِ اللّٰهُمَّ مٰلِكَ الْمُلْكِ تُؤْتِی الْمُلْكَ مَنْ تَشَآءُ وَتَنْزِعُ الْمُلْكَ مِمَّنْ تَشَآءُ وَتُعِزُّ مَنْ تَشَآءُ وَتُذِلُّ مَنْ تَشَآءُ ؕ بِیَدِكَ الْخَیْرُ ؕ اِنَّكَ عَلٰی كُلِّ شَیْءٍ قَدِیْرٌ ۝}$$

That is, O you who is being addressed, declare that: 'O Allah, Lord of sovereignty, You give sovereignty to whomsoever You please; and You take away sovereignty from whomsoever You please. You exalt whomsoever You please and You abase whomsoever You please. In Your hand is all good. You surely have power to do all things.'

This verse reminds us that whenever an individual gains authority, it is a trust from God Himself. This does not mean that every ruler and person in authority—no matter how cruel, corrupt, foul or worthless he might be—is appointed by God as His representative. Rather this verse implies that circumstances that lead one to gain authority are created by God. Thus, if someone attains authority, it is due to him taking advantage of God's created circumstances.

Since authority comes from God, anyone who gains authority or power in this world can at most consider himself as a subordinate and trustee of God. He cannot consider himself to

---

[3] *Sūrah Āl-e-'Imrān*, 3:27, (publishers)

be the absolute ruler or authority. The ultimate authority and decision rests with God Almighty. Any ruler, king, dictator or parliamentarian, who is entrusted with the affairs of a state, is answerable before God for the laws he enacts in this world. If laws promote things that God has forbidden or prohibit things that God has ordained, then such rulers will stand guilty before God Almighty just as insubordinate and rebellious servant is made to stand before his master. Regardless of their status—whether they be a king, dictator or a parliamentarian—they will surely be punished by God Almighty for their actions.

Thus the above-quoted verse does not imply that every person who gains authority is appointed by God Himself. Instead, it means that if a person is given authority within his circle of influence, he must rule within the limits prescribed by God Himself—the ultimate authority. Doing otherwise would be considered sinful. It is true, however, that under certain circumstances, God does directly appoint people in authority, who are noble and just, but their rule is spiritual not worldly.

Injunctions for Those in Authority

The Holy Quran states that some among the rulers are such that:[4]

$$وَإِذَا تَوَلّٰى سَعٰى فِى الْأَرْضِ لِيُفْسِدَ فِيْهَا وَيُهْلِكَ الْحَرْثَ وَالنَّسْلَ ۚ وَاللّٰهُ لَا يُحِبُّ الْفَسَادَ۞$$

---

[4] *Sūrah al-Baqarah*, 2:206, (publishers)

That is, there are many rulers and kings in the world, who when they assume power—that is, when they acquire authority by employing God-given capacities—they run about in the land to create disorder in it instead of serving the country and its inhabitants. Their activities create disturbances and disorder between different tribes, nations and religious groups, and result in economic disruption, cultural degradation, and the ruin of future generations.

This verse points out that there are rulers and kings who gain authority because of God-given faculties. However, once in power, instead of serving their country or its people, and establishing peace and security, they introduce measures that lead to conflict between people of different countries, tribes and religions, and create chaos in the land. They also adopt ways that destroy the country's social and economic fabric and bring ruin to future generations.

The word *ḥarth* in the Quranic verse literally means an 'agricultural crop', but here it is used figuratively with a wider connotation to all resources of economic development and financial well-being. The reference is to the rulers who do not adopt measures appropriate for economic growth and financial improvements of their people, but, instead, make laws that destroy the country's society, its economy and its financial situation. In this way, they create obstacles for the progress of future generations and make laws that deprive them of the capacity and knowledge needed for growth and development. God reminds us: 'Allah loves not disorder'. Thus, He regards such sovereigns and rulers with displeasure, and worthy of divine chastisement.

The conclusion from the above verse is that, according to Islam, the rulers, in the true sense of the word, are those that provide peace, improve economic well-being of their subjects, make their lives secure, and do not squander the country's resources in unnecessary wars resulting in wanton loss of life. In other words, the State is obligated to ensure peace, security and well-being of its citizens.

Justice Among People and Nations

The Holy Quran states at another place:[5]

$$\text{إِنَّ اللَّهَ يَأْمُرُكُمْ أَنْ تُؤَدُّوا الْأَمَانَاتِ إِلَىٰ أَهْلِهَا وَإِذَا حَكَمْتُمْ بَيْنَ النَّاسِ أَنْ تَحْكُمُوا بِالْعَدْلِ ۚ إِنَّ اللَّهَ نِعِمَّا يَعِظُكُمْ بِهِ ۗ إِنَّ اللَّهَ كَانَ سَمِيعًا بَصِيرًا}$$

That is, O people, Allah commands that when you are in a position to make over the trust of authority to someone, you should grant it to those worthy of discharging the responsibility. [Then those who are placed in authority are addressed with the admonition that since they have been elected to positions of authority by the people, it is their duty that] When you make certain decisions, do so with justice. And surely Allah admonishes you! Excellent is that with which Allah admonishes you. Verily Allah is All-Hearing, All-Seeing.

This verse instructs the people that when given the opportunity to choose someone as the ruler, they should select the best candidate for the task, who is capable of discharging the affairs of

---

[5] *Sūrah an-Nisā'*, 4:59, (publishers)

the State with integrity and competence. He should be the best leader, committed to promoting general welfare.

The latter part of the verse, 'And surely excellent is that with which Allah admonishes you!', tells us that divine injunctions are not like those of some rulers who issue orders without due consideration or thought, instructing people to behave one way or the other. Instead, this injunction comes from your Creator and Master and is for your own good and welfare. If you appoint rulers who are good, who appropriately discharge the affairs of the state and understand the importance of the trust reposed in them, then it is all for your own benefit.

If rulers protect people's lives and wealth, make decisions based on justice and fairness, do not discriminate against individuals or communities, treat the weak and the strong equally, maintain order within the State, and do not tread the path of rulers who show favouritism and bias, then they would not only be carrying out God's commandment, but would themselves benefit from this conduct.

The Holy Quran further states 'Allah is All-Hearing, All-Seeing', meaning that God watched as people were trampled upon and destroyed by tyrannical and ruthless rulers who usurped the people's rights. God witnessed this state of affairs and His sense of justice and fair play was aroused as mankind continued to suffer cruelty while the rulers did whatever their whims dictated. Therefore, God decided to give instructions on these matters Himself. When injustice reached its zenith and the people pleaded for mercy with agony that, 'O Lord! Such rulers are being imposed on us who do not grant us our rights.' God then decided that in his next shariah, [religious law] He would ordain that rulers be appointed through election, and only those persons be elected who would act with equity and justice, and were capable of running the affairs of the state. Similarly, God instructed the rulers in his shariah that they must always act with equity and justice, strive constantly to uplift the nation's economic condition, protect the life and property of its citizens, and not discriminate between individuals and nations and not adopt ways that would be detrimental to the development of the country and future generations. Instead, the rulers should always adopt such means and laws that are essential for the country's progress.

Basic Precepts of Governance in Islam

The economic system of Islam requires a specific governance environment, as no system, however good, can be effective outside its appropriate environment. Islam is the first religion of the world that:

- ❖ Advocates a system of representative government, with the capability of candidate as the fundamental criterion for election.
- ❖ Defines authority as a trust, not a right.
- ❖ Declares that the basic goal of government must be to protect honour, life and property of citizens.
- ❖ Enjoins the rulers to judge amongst individuals and communities with absolute justice and impartiality, reminding them that they are ultimately answerable before God.

In short, there is no room for hereditary kingship in Islam. It unequivocally declares that: 'Verily, Allah commands you to make over the trusts to those entitled to them'. Hence, Islam does not approve of hereditary kingship. Instead, Islam enjoins that the trust of governance be given by elections to people who are most capable of carrying that burden. It is the duty of Muslims to evaluate carefully candidates' capabilities and entrust the authority to govern to the best amongst them.

As long as Muslims abided by this injunction of the Holy Quran, they elected their rulers who met the prescribed criteria. In the future, too, when Muslims come to follow the injunction of the Holy Quran, they would be obligated to hold elections to choose people to run the affairs of the country. Moreover, they would be expected to abstain from electing someone solely on the basis of his family background, influence, or wealth. They should also not elect someone simply because he is backed by a powerful group. The basic consideration for electing someone should be his ability to manage the country's affairs. At the same time, God enjoins the elected rulers that they rule with equity and justice. This was the spirit that kept Muslims inclined towards justice and democratic norms despite the rise of kingship among them.

Historical Illustrations of Islamic Precepts of Governance

PRAYER OF MALEK SHAH

In his *[History of the] Decline and Fall of the Roman Empire*, the renowned Christian author, Gibbon, narrates the story of a Turkish king, Malek Shah, who was only a youth when his father (Alp Arsalan) passed away. Following the demise of his father, three other individuals—Malek Shah's brother, an uncle and a cousin— rose as claimants to the throne, leading to a civil war. Nizamud-Din Toosi who was Malek Shah's vizier [minister] and happened to be a Shia, persuaded Malek Shah to visit the tomb of Imam Musa Riza to offer prayers. After the prayers, Malek Shah asked his vizier, 'what had been the object of his secret petition'? The vizier replied that he prayed to Allah 'That your [Malek Shah's] arms may be crowned with victory.' 'For my part (replied the generous Malek), I implored the Lord of hosts that he would take from me my life and crown, if my brother be more worthy than myself to reign over the Moslems.' Gibbon, is a Christian historian, deeply prejudiced against Islam, yet he was compelled to say regarding this incident that historically: 'it would not be easy to extract a sentiment more pure and magnanimous than is contained in the saying of the Turkish prince'.

Where did this spirit come from? How was it embedded in the Muslims' hearts that governance was not the personal right of any individual, that it was a trust that a country's people confer upon the most deserving, and that it was the ruler's duty to govern with justice and fulfil the rights of individuals? Such noble ideology and splendid examples exist amongst the Muslims because the Holy Quran from the very beginning taught Muslims that authority is a trust that should only be handed over, by elections, to the deserving person. It cannot be seized by some as their hereditary right, nor can it be passed on according to any criteria other than merit.

Similarly, the person who is granted this trust must fulfil all the obligations associated with it. Anyone who does not fulfil these obligations shall stand before God as a condemned man. Muslims always kept in their minds the following verse:[6]

$$...تُؤَدُّوا الْأَمٰنٰتِ اِلٰٓى اَهْلِهَا...$$

That is, only those individuals should be given this trust who are worthy of it and have the capability to deal with administrative issues.

The people who were given this trust always remained mindful of the Quranic injunction that they must rule with integrity and justice. They knew that if they were unmindful of justice and were not scrupulously honest, or otherwise became unworthy of the trust reposed in them, they would be answerable before God to face retribution for their transgression.

ANGUISH OF ḤAḌRAT UMAR[RA] AT HIS DEATHBED

The above-mentioned Quranic injunctions were so deeply instilled in the personality of Ḥaḍrat Umar[ra] that others might

---

[6] *Sūrah an-Nisā'*, 4:59, (publishers)

find it astounding. He was the second Khalīfah of Islam, who made tremendous sacrifices for the progress of Islam and Muslims. Even those European writers who routinely criticise the Holy Prophet[sa]—accusing him (God forbid) of dishonesty in his dealings—cannot but admit that the way Ḥaḍrat Abu Bakr[ra] and Ḥaḍrat Umar[ra] worked tirelessly and selflessly in the service of mankind is unparalleled in history. These authors are especially complimentary to Ḥaḍrat Umar[ra]. According to them, he was a man who worked with total dedication day and night to spread the message of Islam and to advance the Muslim cause. However, despite his tireless effort, countless sacrifices, and the pain and suffering he endured for the sake of Muslims, what was his assessment about himself? He remained mindful of the following verse that: [7]

$$...\text{اِنَّ اللّٰهَ يَأْمُرُكُمْ اَنْ تُؤَدُّوا الْاَمٰنٰتِ اِلٰٓى اَهْلِهَا}...$$

And:

$$...\text{وَاِذَا حَكَمْتُمْ بَيْنَ النَّاسِ اَنْ تَحْكُمُوْا بِالْعَدْلِ}...$$

That is, when you are appointed to an office of trust by the decree of God, and your countrymen and brethren appoint you to the responsibility of governance, it is incumbent upon you to rule with justice.

---

[7] Verily, Allah commands you to make over the trusts to those entitled to them. *Sūrah an-Nisā'*, 4:59, (publishers)

How painful is the following episode of his life! When a person—out of foolishness and misperception that Ḥaḍrat Umar[ra] had been unjust—fatally stabbed him, Ḥaḍrat Umar[ra] lay in anguish on his deathbed with the following words on his lips:

> O my Lord: I ask for no reward: only be pleased to call me not to account for my shortcomings. (*Usdul-Ghābah*, vol. 4, p. 75)

His only thought was: 'O Lord! You gave me this authority and trust. I do not know if I truly fulfilled my duty. Now the time of my death is near and I am about to leave this world and return to You. O my Lord! I do not ask for any compensation for my services and I do not seek any reward. Instead, I only seek your mercy. If I have done any wrong in discharging the responsibilities that were assigned to me, I seek your forgiveness.'

Ḥaḍrat Umar[ra] was a man of such high calibre that it is hard to find other examples in history that come close to his sense of equity and justice, yet he died under the weight of the Quranic injunction:[8]

$$ ...وَإِذَا حَكَمْتُمْ بَيْنَ النَّاسِ اَنْ تَحْكُمُوا بِالْعَدْلِ... $$

Even at his death he was restless and troubled. He was not satisfied with all the services that he had rendered for the betterment of his people and for advancing the cause of Islam. He had given such

---

[8] *Sūrah an-Nisā'*, 4:59, (publishers)

tremendous service for his people that not only his own people, but others also recognized them. His services were appreciated during his own time but also thirteen hundred years later and by people who were otherwise inclined to attacking his master. Yet, all of these services were nothing in Umar's[ra] own eyes and he restlessly pleaded to God: 'I was given a trust but I do not know if I fulfilled that trust as it was meant to be fulfilled. Therefore, I beseech You to forgive my faults and save me from the punishment.'

I have deemed it necessary to describe at length the general environment needed for establishing the Islamic economic system, because no matter how good a seed is, it would not mature into a tree unless the soil was appropriate for its growth and nourishment. On the other hand, even an ordinary seed, in a nourishing environment, could grow and mature into a plant. Thus, the general environment described above is the precondition for the Islamic economic system intended to serve public interest.

Types of Economic Systems in the World

The economic systems prevalent in the world can be classified into three types. There is one type of economic system that is not governed by any specified rules and regulations, and can be called a 'system' only for the sake of convenience. Some nations and countries never spelled out how their economic system would be run and had no specific plan or policy towards that end. Such societies do not distinguish between individual and national goals, and in the absence of a set policy, adopt any idea that appears convenient or practical.

The second system is nationalistic in its approach, that is, one where nations seek only to maximize their collective national interests.

The third system is individualistic, i.e., it gives individuals an opportunity to work on their own for the betterment and progress of their country. Workers as well as owners of capital are permitted to struggle for their rights and pursue their self-interest. Employees have the right to negotiate their wages and benefits with the management, which in turn is expected to institute clear rules and regulations governing workers. Thus the emphasis in this system is on the individual.

These are the three basic economic systems that exist in the world today. The first system is not bound by any definite laws or rules; the second system is nationalistic in its approach, while the third is driven by individualism. Islam does not accept the first system at all, for the Islamic system is based on prescribed principles and laws, which people are enjoined to follow. Islam relies on purpose and wisdom, and does not approve of indiscriminate adoption of economic policies. A system without well-designed laws is akin to feeding off of wild vegetation that grows on its own. Islamic system, on the other hand, can be compared to a farmer who follows a set routine for sowing seeds, irrigation, and nurturing plants. He knows what to keep in his orchard and what to throw out.

Teachings of Islam for Establishing a Just Society

The foundation of Islamic teachings that I described earlier is essential for understanding its economic philosophy. I elaborated on those concepts because the Islamic economic system cannot succeed in the absence of its necessary environment.

As I have already mentioned, Islam does not recognize a system that is not based on law. Instead, Islam presents a path that is a combination of the other two systems (nationalistic and individualistic). As such, the fundamentals of the Islamic economic system are the same as those of Islam itself, as mentioned above.

Basic Precepts of Islam Regarding Wealth

The Islamic point of view in regard to the sources of wealth is expressed in the Holy Quran:[9]

$$\text{هُوَ الَّذِىْ خَلَقَ لَكُمْ مَّا فِى الْأَرْضِ جَمِيْعًا} ...$$

That is, everything that is found in the world has been created by Allah for the benefit of mankind.

Mountains, rivers, mineral wealth and other means of human progress are mankind's collective property, and we all have a share in this collective wealth. All these natural resources provide

---

[9] *Sūrah al-Baqarah*, 2:30, (publishers)

electricity, gold, silver, and other precious metals as well as drugs and chemicals that are used to treat illnesses. There is limitless variety of produced goods, some for personal consumption, some for industry as raw materials, and some are traded internationally.

God reminds us that everything has been created for the benefit of mankind. No individual can lay exclusive claim upon these resources, whether it is a Pharaoh, a Hitler, a Churchill or a Roosevelt. Everything that has been created is for the benefit of the entire human race, including the rulers and the ruled, the high and the low, the superior and the subservient. No one may claim that God has created these things only for his own personal use. The Quran tells us that 'I have created this for you' and that we are all collective claimants of His creation.

Islamic Injunction on the Use of Wealth

The Quran spells out the following principle regarding the true purpose of wealth: [10]

...اٰتُوهُمْ مِّنْ مَّالِ اللّٰهِ الَّذِىٓ اٰتٰىكُمْ...

[And give them out of the wealth of Allah which He has bestowed upon you.]

The pronoun 'them' in this passage, as shown by the context, stands for slaves, i.e. prisoners of war who are not in a position to ransom

---

[10] *Sūrah an-Nūr*, 24:34, (publishers)

themselves either out of their own personal and family means, or with the help of the government or country they had fought for.

In such situations, Quran instructs us that we should help the prisoners of war by providing them with resources that they can employ to make money and use it to procure their own release by paying the required ransom. We are thus taught that if we are holding some unfortunate people, whom the vicissitudes of life had deprived them of the power to stand on their own feet, they should be given the benefit of a portion of our resources, which really belong to God and in which every creature of God holds a share.

Similarly, the verse quoted above instructs Muslim rulers and kings that the wealth, which God has given them, does not solely belong to them, but all of mankind has a share in it. Even if they capture prisoners of war who are so unfortunate that their own countrymen and family abandon them and show little interest in getting them freed (possibly because people back home wish to usurp the prisoners' property), it remains the duty of Muslims in authority not to abandon them. In such a situation, they are urged to spend a portion of their wealth to set the prisoners free, since 'your wealth is not yours but belongs to God, and your prisoner is created by the same God who created you.''

These references demonstrate that: Firstly, according to Islam, the world's wealth belongs to all mankind. Secondly, the real master of all wealth is only God Almighty. Man is therefore not free to dispose of his wealth in any way he deems fit; what he can do is circumscribed by God's prescribed limits.

We learn from the Holy Quran that this basic principle of ownership of wealth is an age-old truth, proclaimed by every Prophet of God. The Holy Quran refers to Ḥaḍrat Shu'aib[as] when he warned his people against usurping the rights of others, against injustice, and against adopting ways of earning and spending wealth that led to strife. The people's response was:[11]

$$...اَصَلوٰتُكَ تَأْمُرُكَ اَنْ نَتْرُكَ مَا يَعْبُدُ اٰبَآؤُنَآ اَوْاَنْ نَفْعَلَ فِيْٓ اَمْوَالِنَا مَا نَشٰٓؤُا ؕ اِنَّكَ لَاَنْتَ الْحَلِيْمُ الرَّشِيْدُ۞$$

That is, O Shu'aib! What is the matter with you. The money is ours, the wealth is ours, the property is ours, and we feel that we can give it to whomsoever we please, and we can keep it from whomsoever we please; spend it wherever we please and not spend it wherever we please. Who are you to intrude upon such matters? This wealth is not yours to decide where to distribute or spend; it is ours, and we maintain the choice to spend it however we please. Has your mind become perplexed from offering prayer after prayer that you are now interfering in our financial affairs and telling us that if we spend in this way it shall be virtuous, and if we spend in that way it shall lead to punishment? Whence have you acquired the right to counsel and teach us?

Then the people taunted, 'Thou art indeed very intelligent and right-minded,' i.e., who are you to preach in favour of the poor! That is, we accept that you are intelligent and right-minded, but now you claim that you can tell us how we should behave? We reject this claim of yours.

This clearly explains that the teachings of the Holy Quran regarding wealth are the same as were presented by the earlier

---

[11] *Sūrah Hūd,* 11:88, (publishers)

Prophets. They did not consider human beings entirely free to earn and spend as they pleased. They believed that all wealth belonged to God ultimately and that spending it against His will was unlawful.

Exhortations for Uplifting of the Poor as a Necessity for National Progress

Islam ordained sympathy for the poor and downtrodden and their uplift was a major concern at its very inception. A study of the chapters of the Holy Quran that were revealed in the beginning of Islam shows that the most dominant message in these verses is to support and uplift the poor. Muslims are told that if they desired national progress and God's pleasure then they must try to help the poor and alleviate their sufferings.

Although at that point other injunctions of Islam—such as, how to pray, how to trade, how to judge, how to deal with each other, the rights of husbands and wives, the rights of rulers and ruled, and the rights of employers and employees—were not yet revealed, the Quran drew attention to supporting and uplifting the poor. The people were reminded that nations that did not help their poor and ignored the rights of the downtrodden were destined to be destroyed and would face God's wrath.

EMPHASIS ON AMELIORATING THE CONDITIONS OF THE POOR IN EARLY ISLAMIC TEACHINGS.

History shows that the first chapter to be revealed was *Sūrah al-'Alaq* (Chapter 96). The opening verses of this *Sūrah* were revealed in the first instance, followed by a gradual revelation of the whole chapter, spread over a short time period. Four of the chapters that followed immediately after this *Sūrah* have been called a 'soliloquy' by Sir William Muir, a well-respected European Orientalist, who was, at one time, the Lieutenant Governor of U.P. He held that these chapters gave expression to the thoughts that filled the mind of the Holy Prophet[sa] prior to his claim of Prophethood.

According to Sir William Muir these four chapters are *Sūrah al-Balad, Sūrah ash-Shams, Sūrah al-Lail and Sūrah aḍ-Ḍuḥā*. Muslim scholars believe that these four chapters were revealed after *Sūrah al-'Alaq*, and historical evidence supports this view. However, Muir was of the opinion that these four chapters were revealed prior to *Sūrah al-'Alaq*. His argument was based on the thesis that *Sūrah al-'Alaq* begins with the Arabic word *iqra'*, meaning, 'read'. Thus it must be the case—according to Muir—that there were chapters that had been already revealed and were to be read.

In any event, these four chapters of the Holy Quran are the very earliest chapters according to Islamic history, and according to Muir they were revealed even before the Holy Prophet[sa] claimed that he has been commissioned as a Prophet. When we look at these four chapters, we find that three of them declare taking care of the poor to be necessary for salvation and national progress. They also instruct the rich to reform themselves. For example, it is stated in *Sūrah al-Balad*:[12]

يَقُولُ اَهْلَكْتُ مَالًا لُّبَدًا ۞ اَيَحْسَبُ اَنْ لَّمْ يَرَهٗٓ اَحَدٌ ۞ اَلَمْ نَجْعَلْ لَّهٗ عَيْنَيْنِ ۞ وَ لِسَانًا وَّ شَفَتَيْنِ ۞ وَهَدَيْنٰهُ النَّجْدَيْنِ ۞ فَلَا اقْتَحَمَ الْعَقَبَةَ ۞ وَمَآ اَدْرٰىكَ مَا الْعَقَبَةُ ۞ فَكُّ رَقَبَةٍ ۞ اَوْ اِطْعٰمٌ فِيْ يَوْمٍ ذِيْ مَسْغَبَةٍ ۞ يَّتِيْمًا ذَا مَقْرَبَةٍ ۞ اَوْ مِسْكِيْنًا ذَا مَتْرَبَةٍ ۞ ثُمَّ كَانَ مِنَ الَّذِيْنَ اٰمَنُوْا وَتَوَاصَوْا بِالصَّبْرِ وَتَوَاصَوْا بِالْمَرْحَمَةِ ۞

Allah the Almighty says: 'Every rich man in the world says, اَهْلَكْتُ مَالًا لُّبَدًا... 'I am very rich and I have spent enormous wealth without any concern for the amount spent and therefore, I am entitled to honour and respect in the public.' The Arabic word *lubad* in this verse means 'heap after heap', and this is an accurate description of the scale at which wealth is wasted by the rich in worthless pursuits.'

Then He says: اَيَحْسَبُ اَنْ لَّمْ يَرَهٗٓ اَحَدٌ 'Does such a foolish one think that no one sees him?' i.e., by spending countless amounts he thinks that he has done a favour to the country, but people can see that he is doing it for show and is not motivated by sympathy and love for the poor. If he had those feelings, he would have spread his enormous expenditure over many days for the benefit and feeding of the poor, but he totally lacked such motives. His only motivation was to be known for his wealth. 'Does he imagine that no one sees him?' He is totally wrong. The world is not blind and stupid. It is clear to

---

[12] *Sūrah al-Balad*, 90:7–18, (publishers)

everyone that his spending was not for human welfare, but for self-glorification.

اَلَمْ نَجْعَلْ لَّهُ عَيْنَيْنِ Then He adds: 'Have We not given him two eyes?'—he should have used them to look at conditions prevailing around him. The poor are dying of hunger with no one to care for them, but he is spending heaps for his glory. Had he not been granted eyes, with which he could see the conditions surrounding him.

And then He says: وَلِسَانًا وَشَفَتَيْنِ 'And he had been given a tongue and two lips', with which he could have discussed the situation and the proper uses of money.

The verse continues: وَهَدَيْنَاهُ النَّجْدَيْنِ 'And We have pointed out to him the two highways' of material and spiritual progress i.e. placed within his nature the impulse to seek the ways of attaining nearness to Allah as well as practising human sympathy and concern. But he did not employ any of the three means, and spent his wealth without a valid purpose. Therefore, he only wasted the money.

Then Allah the Almighty says: فَلَا اقْتَحَمَ الْعَقَبَةَ 'But he attempted not the ascent courageously'—despite having eyes to see the condition of the poor, and having the tongue and the lips to enquire about it, and having an ingrain feeling for the love of God and humanity—'he attempted not the ascent courageously.' Like an overweight man, he got tired and failed to scale the heights—i.e. kept spending his wealth for show rather than the real purpose of achieving human welfare through it.

There are many other examples of wasteful spending. For example, some pleasure-seekers spend a fortune on dancing women, others, for lack of alternatives, spend it on gatherings of poetry recitals. There may be a poor widow in their backyard holding in her lap her hungry and crying children all night, but the rich give little thought to feeding the orphans, as they care more for their fame. However, God declares that they are not spending their money but rather wasting it.

Then Allah the Almighty says: وَمَآ أَدْرَىٰكَ مَا ٱلْعَقَبَةُ 'Do you know what the uphill ascent is?' and then goes on to explain that it is the feeling of sympathy that yearns to help and free that slave who toils in alien soil away from his family and home. It is the feeding of the poor and the hungry, instead of wasting money on feasts for the rich, sometimes involving slaughter of hundreds of camels in one day. In times of drought and extreme cold, when food is scarce, it is the caring of the downtrodden, the feeding of the hungry and the clothing of the naked. It is the feeding of the orphan, instead of wasting money on lavish dinners, or gambling or wasteful sports.

The verse 'feeding of an orphan, near of kin' does not mean that one should only feed the orphan who is a relative. As it is, even the most miserly person would feed an orphan who was related to him. Instead, this verse highlights the fact that there are two types of orphans. First there are orphans who do not have any relatives. These orphans are so helpless and friendless that at times even the most stonehearted of men would feel sympathy and feed them. But then there is a second category of orphans, who may have close relatives, such as, brothers, sisters, uncles, etc. People tend to pay less attention to such orphans, as they are held to have family to support them. However, God expects such a high standard of compassion that, even for an orphan with relatives, we should feel such love in our hearts that we consider him or her as our own kin.

The last part of the verse asks why 'a poor man lying in the dust' was not fed. The Arabic expression *dha-matrabah*, or 'lying in the dust', in this verse implies the kind of extreme poverty that reduces one to near non-existence. Persistent destitution can deprive one of even the ability and energy to raise a voice. There are beggars who go from door to door seeking relief. Some of them beg insistently and refuse to take no for an answer. Others raise hue and cry in protest, and organize themselves to press the government and the rich to help them. However, God expects us to have such sympathy and love that we must seek out the helpless poor who do not even have the capacity to protest and beg at someone's door. Such a person is not a member of a 'trade union' of beggars; his lips remain sealed even though his stomach may be empty; he remains hidden away in sickness and grief; he is friendless with no hope or energy left.

Islam expects the rich to reach out to such hopeless poor and strive to heal their bruised hearts. Islam expects the rich to achieve such heights of moral advancement that, after doing everything in their power in the service of the poor, they do not regard themselves as superior for being charitable. Instead, Islam expects the rich to remain humble before God and constantly prod their hearts to ascertain if they have truly fulfilled their duty towards the poor. The rich must not remind the poor of their help, nor should they consider it as a favour to the recipient. Rather, they should constantly engage in self-examination if they have fulfilled their God-given obligations.

The next verse ...وَتَوَاصَوْا بِالصَّبْرِ... 'And exhort one another to be steadfast' describes the next stage on this 'uphill road.' It indicates that: beyond helping individuals, one seeks to address the troubles of the entire nation.[13] One should not blindly indulge in the life of ease while the poor are living a life of distress. These days, because of rationing, the rich are able to get the goods while the poor are left empty handed. The rich must not content themselves in just helping the poor; they should also persuade their friends and relatives to do likewise. Everyone should collectively work to improve the nation's well-being and support each other in that effort. The next stage is that, despite all the good works, they are still left feeling that nothing has been done. And in that spirit, they must continue to remind one's fellow beings the importance of helping and caring for the weak and the poor and continue such exhortations up to the last breath of their lives.

This teaching belongs to the earliest period of Islam, when the Holy Quran had just begun to be revealed and details of its commandments had yet to come. It was a time when even the people of Makkah were scarcely aware of Islam. Sir William Muir maintains that these were the thoughts of Holy Prophet[sa] and tendencies that led him eventually to claim (God forbid) Prophethood. We believe that these teachings comprise the earliest revelations to which applied the Divine command embodied in the word *iqra'* (read)—i.e. convey these teachings to the people. Nevertheless, these teachings, revealed in the very early days of Islam, make clear that while individual freedom and struggle for personal material progress are permitted, it is not acceptable that a few individuals live a life of luxury while others suffer in pain and misery.

---

[13] *Sūrah al-Balad*, 90:18, (publishers)

Measures to End the Institution of Slavery

It should be remembered that the basic source of unnatural and iniquitous treatment—which existed since time immemorial and which Islam brought to an end—was the institution of slavery. It may be not be possible for people today to appreciate the intimate link between slavery and the rise of global commerce and economy; indeed, this is the reason that Islam put a stop to the practice of slavery.

Role Played by Slave Labour in World Economy

Before the inception of Islam—in fact, even after its rise—the institution of slavery prevailed over a large part of the world. On examining the history of ancient Rome, Greece, Egypt and Persia, we find that slave labour was used as the instrument of economic progress in all of these countries.

Slavery was made possible basically through two channels. One way was when countries at war with neighbouring states captured the citizens of their opponents and turned them into slaves. For example, when the opportunity arose, the Romans would capture the Persians as slaves, or the other way around. Thus, each side would enslave people of the other side, expecting thereby to deal a blow to the opponent's political power. The second way to enslave people was to capture women and children from the backward parts of the world. While the first means of enslaving people was adopted at opportune occasions, the second method became a sustained practice over time.

In fact, that approach to slavery continued well into the 18th century when hoards of West Africans were brought over into the United States. Although slavery no longer exists in that country, some 20–30 million Americans are descendents of people who were brought as slaves.

The main motivation behind slavery in advanced countries was to further their economic might through cheap slave labour. The slaves were exploited in different ways. They were assigned to work in factories, or ships, or any other work involving heavy manual tasks required for economic development. Similarly, slave labour was used on plantations in order to minimise production costs and to maximize profit.

Prohibition of Unjust Forms of Slavery

In both of the above-mentioned forms, slavery denied equality in treatment to a cross-section of mankind. Islam categorically prohibited both channels of enslaving people. The Holy Quran says: [14]

مَا كَانَ لِنَبِيٍّ أَنْ يَكُونَ لَهُ أَسْرَىٰ حَتَّىٰ يُثْخِنَ فِي الْأَرْضِ ۚ تُرِيدُونَ عَرَضَ الدُّنْيَا ۖ وَاللَّهُ يُرِيدُ الْآخِرَةَ ۗ وَاللَّهُ عَزِيزٌ حَكِيمٌ ۝

Meaning that: It was not lawful for any Prophet before you, nor is it for you, to take prisoners without engaging in a war. If there is a

---

[14] *Sūrah al-Anfāl*, 8:68, (publishers)

war—and that too, religious—prisoners can be captured in the battlefield.

The condition laid down in this verse does not permit anyone to imprison the civilian population of any country where war has not been declared. Nor does it permit enslaving any citizen of the opponent who has not been part of the attacking force. The imprisonment of those who actively engage in combat is allowed because they would otherwise go back to join forces in attack.

Then Allah says in these verses that: ...تُرِيْدُوْنَ عَرَضَ الدُّنْيَا... 'You desire the frail goods of this world' meaning: O Muslims, do you desire to behave like other nations and enslave their people to augment your power ...وَاللهُ يُرِيْدُ الْآخِرَةَ... nay, Allah does not want you to follow other nations. He wants to guide you to the course that is better for you in the end and entitles you to win Allah's pleasure. God reminds Muslims that nearness to God is better than any worldly gain. And God decrees that it is better for you that you do not take any prisoners except when war is imposed on you.

This rule was strictly enforced in the early days of Islam. During the reign of Ḥaḍrat Umar[ra], a deputation from Yemen came and complained that, before the advent of Islam, they had been made into slaves without any cause by a neighbouring Christian tribe. Ḥaḍrat Umar[ra] replied that though the event took place before the Muslims were in power, he would look into the case and have them set free if their complaint was borne out by facts. In contrast to this enlightened Islamic stand, the Europeans continued to use slavery for advancing their trade and agriculture until the nineteenth century.

There is no doubt that some instances of the un-Islamic custom of slavery can be found in Islamic history; but slavery was never practised to promote domestic industry or trade.

Exhortations for Freeing the Prisoners of War

With respect specifically to the prisoners of war, Islam decrees:[15]

$$...إِمَّا مَنًّا بَعْدُ وَإِمَّا فِدَآءً...$$

That is: Then afterwards either release them as a favour or by taking ransom.

No third option is given. The captor can either release prisoners of war out of compassion and rest assured that God is pleased with his action or if financial hardship does not allow the captors to set prisoners of war free without recompense, then it is permissible to charge the customary ransom for release. However, what happens if neither the prisoner nor his country or family have the resources to pay ransom? Islam then allows the prisoner to pay his ransom in regular instalments and thereby earn his freedom. Allah the Almighty says:[16]

$$...وَالَّذِينَ يَبْتَغُونَ الْكِتَابَ مِمَّا مَلَكَتْ أَيْمَانُكُمْ فَكَاتِبُوهُمْ$$
$$إِنْ عَلِمْتُمْ فِيهِمْ خَيْرًا وَآتُوهُم مِّن مَّالِ اللهِ الَّذِي آتَاكُمْ...$$

---

[15] *Sūrah Muḥammad*, 47:5, (publishers)
[16] *Sūrah an-Nūr*, 24:34, (publishers)

That is: If you have a prisoner whom you cannot release as a favour, and his relatives can not pay the ransom, then if such a prisoner desires a deed of manumission in writing, write it for them if you know any good in them; and give them out of the wealth of Allah which He has bestowed upon you.

In situations where the slave is unable to pay the ransom, this verse enjoins that a bond be executed between a master and his slave, which binds the latter to pay the ransom in agreed instalments. After this bond has been executed, the slave is immediately restored to freedom, and he is free to take up any trade he may have an aptitude for. As a beautiful, crowning gesture of goodwill, the master, out of his own assets, is directed to provide the prisoner with some capital to start him on the new venture. Out of these earnings, the master is not entitled to anything beyond the agreed fixed instalment.

When one considers the Islamic teachings regarding slavery, it becomes clear that Islam leaves absolutely no avenue open for any person to make another person a slave. Even when prisoners of war are taken, the captors are encouraged to set them free as a favour or else they must be set free on payment of a reasonable ransom. If there is a prisoner who cannot ransom himself and his friends or his government take no steps towards paying his ransom, he can gain freedom by giving an undertaking that would enable him to pay his ransom in instalments out of his earnings. Destitute prisoners are even helped with some capital to enable them to earn their livelihood and gain freedom. If in the presence of such extraordinary concessions, a prisoner does not avail himself of the opportunities offered, it can only mean that he finds his 'bondage' among Muslims more agreeable than free life among his own people.

Careful consideration of these injunctions makes it obvious that Islam leaves no room for anyone to enslave another free person. The first commandment is to free the slaves as a favour, without any ransom. If that is not possible, Islam enjoins freeing the prisoners with an appropriate ransom. If a prisoner cannot arrange for the ransom from his own resources, or from his relatives, he can execute a bond and would, for all practical purposes, be totally free owing nothing more than the agreed instalment.

The slave who stabbed and martyred Ḥaḍrat Umar[ra] was himself set free according to the ransom guidelines given above. One day, the slave approached the Muslim who he lived with, and proposed payment of a fixed instalment of ransom out of his income in exchange for his freedom. A contract was signed that mandated the slave to earn his freedom by paying the agreed instalments. However, one day he complained to the Khalīfah that his instalment was too heavy and that it should be reduced. On investigation, Ḥaḍrat Umar[ra] found that the man's income was many times greater than the agreed instalment. His application was therefore rejected, which made him furious. He thought that justice had been denied to him on racial grounds, as he was a Persian while his former master was an Arab. So the next day he stabbed Ḥaḍrat Umar[ra] with a dagger, who was martyred because of the wounds.

To sum up, Islam gives a right to any prisoner of war to gain his freedom by paying ransom in cash or in agreed instalments. If he is then unable to embark upon an economic activity for lack of capital, the master or the government is enjoined to assist him in procuring the needed funds to gain his freedom.

Fair Treatment of Prisoners

Islam instructs that, when working at the master's home, a prisoner of war must not be given tasks beyond his capacity. If the task is too onerous for the prisoner to do by himself, the master should help him. In any case, he must not be abused. If he is a freedman, working for wages, he should be paid promptly. If the master happens to physically hit a freedman, he has the right to lodge a petition with *qaḍā* [Islamic judicial system] and sue his master for compensation. A servant, who has not yet been freed, can also go to a court of law, for physical abuse. If the complaint is justified, the courts are instructed in such cases to determine that the master is not fit to keep the prisoner, and grant him freedom.

A person possessing prisoners is instructed to feed them the same food as he eats and to clothe them in the manner he clothes himself. It is no wonder that many prisoners of war in Muslim hands refused to go back to their own people. They felt that if they went back home, they might not get the same quality of food as they got as prisoners and their quality of life would actually be worse. Thus, when Muslims became rulers, prisoners of war often refused to return home, even though they were offered payment of their ransom to gain their freedom. This was so because they realized that their life was more comfortable as 'slaves' than as free men back home. If, under such circumstances, a few men chose to remain slaves, who may object?

Slavery and Economics

Although the subject of my address today is not slavery, economics and slavery are inextricably woven together in human history. The development of Siberia in Russia was dependent on the work of serfs and political prisoners. Similarly, the United States of America developed because of the hard work of millions of Africans brought across from West Africa. America today takes pride in its wealth and economic might, but it owes a debt of gratitude to the slaves. Similarly Greek and Roman history tells us that their commerce and industry was for the most part based on slave labour. It is same for ancient Egypt. The economic development in France and Spain two or three hundred years ago was also mainly due to slave labour. Thus, slavery and world economy are intertwined in history no matter where we look. But Islam put a ban on this institution from its inception and pronounced that the development achieved thereby could not be considered moral or praiseworthy.

Impact of Religion Upon the Economic Systems

Before discussing the prevailing economic systems in the world, I wish to point out that any religion that believes in the life after death has to firmly uphold the individual's right to economic freedom.

The fact is that the world contains two kinds of nations: those who believe in religion and those who don't. The latter may adopt any economic system that appeals to their reason. However, those who follow religion would insist upon an economic system that does not bear adversely on the life in the Hereafter. From this perspective, religions that believe in the life Hereafter must insist on individual choice and freedom. It is only then that a person's good actions will find him a place in heaven, where he will attain God's nearness, cognition and pleasure. God's Holiness will protect him and free him of the weaknesses that afflicted him in this world. The nonbelievers may dismiss this conviction as false, but believers in the Hereafter will always give preference to the permanent life in the Hereafter in contrast to the temporary abode here on earth. The idea of spiritual merit in the life to come is fundamentally dependent upon virtuous acts performed voluntarily in this world. These voluntary acts turn life in this world into a field where you cultivate the spiritual seed and gather its fruits in the life to come. A farmer would not plant a seed that gave no yield; human actions performed under duress are similar to the seed that remains barren in the next life. However virtuous a person's actions may seem on the surface, they yield no reward if done under compulsion. Meritorious life in the Hereafter is wholly dependent on good deeds done in this world voluntarily. Those who believe in the Hereafter can never support a system that compels humans to behave in a specified way, for in a system based on compulsion, the field of moral excellence and virtue is greatly constricted. A believer therefore must out of necessity demand an economic system where he is free to choose, except in areas where state intervention is unavoidable.

The Islamic Economic System

Upholding Individual Enterprise

It should be kept in mind that of all religions, Islam places greatest emphasis on the life after death. As such, Islam insists that the economic order should allow the greatest scope to individual enterprise. For an individual, by pursuing his will, has the possibility of improving his place in the life to come. The Islamic view is that if human life were reduced to a succession of compulsory acts, it would preclude free choice and a person could not be held accountable for his actions after death. For example, if a Muslim were compelled by the government to do a good deed, then in the Hereafter he could not claim credit for it. He would be told that it was his government, rather than him, that was responsible for his good deed. It therefore follows that a true Muslim, who understands the fundamentals of his faith, would never accept, as a matter of principle, the suppression of individual freedom.

It follows naturally from the above that Islam, in seeking to establish a fair and just economic order, would proceed to do so on the basis of two fundamental principles.

Voluntary Efforts to Rectify Inequities

The first principle is that inequities in the distribution of resources and means of production should be rectified through voluntary sacrifices on the part of members of society. On the one hand, this would contribute to the economic well-being of society; and on the other it would provide an opportunity to make a provision for the life to come. This is why the Holy Prophet[sa] has said that a man who puts a morsel of food into his wife's mouth with a desire to earn merit in the sight of God, does a deed equal in virtue to giving alms.

The above example is an act in which the husband's own desire plays a part. He is fond of his wife and derives pleasure from caring for her. However, if his motive includes the desire to please God and to gain His nearness, he can turn his domestic obligations into a virtuous deed. He would enjoy the food as before, and his wife would appreciate the clothes he gives her as before. But once he does all this because God loves those who take care of their wives, then not only will he get satisfaction from his own act, but he can also expect a reward from God for doing something for His pleasure.

Wealth Created by God for the Benefit of All

The second basic principle is that all wealth belongs to God, which He has created for the benefit of entire humanity. Therefore, if certain economic problems cannot be corrected through voluntary actions mentioned above, then legal means should be adopted to rectify such situations and bring them in line with the divine will.

Balance Between Individual Freedom and State Intervention

The essence of the economic system of Islam lies in an appropriate combination of individual freedom with state intervention. It allows state intervention to a certain extent, but it also provides for individual freedom. A proper balance between these two defines the Islamic economic system. Individual freedom is granted to enable persons to build up assets and spend them voluntarily in order to gain the spiritual benefits in the life to come. State intervention, on the other hand, is provided in order to protect the poor from economic exploitation by the wealthy.

The state intervention is deemed essential for putting in place certain safeguards against harming the weaker sections of society, while individual freedom is deemed essential for a healthy competition among individuals and for enabling them to make provisions for the life Hereafter. Individuals are given full opportunity to voluntarily serve humanity and earn merit in the life Hereafter. Individual freedom thus opens up endless possibilities of progress through the force of healthy competition. At the same time, judicious state intervention is provided so that the economic system is not based on brutality and injustice and hindrances to economic progress of any section of society are avoided.

It should now be easier to understand that religions that believe in the hereafter in general, and Islam in particular, do not view the issue in simple economic terms, but from a religious, moral and economic perspective. Religion does not seek a purely economic solution because such a solution might interfere with the moral and religious aspects of life, which would be unacceptable. A nonbeliever is of course free to view economic problems in isolation. But a religious person would not judge an economic system from purely an economic perspective. He would demand an economic system that also respects his moral and religious requirements.

After this introduction, let me state that keeping in view the two principles stated above, Islam leaves the individual free to follow any trade or profession. However, Islam also specifies certain limits on individual freedom, which while not interfering with his legitimate aspirations to excel, deter him from taking undue advantage of his freedom or pushing it to dangerous lengths.

It should be remembered that some of the defects that are associated with economic competition are rooted in certain selfish streaks in human nature. For example, a person may set his heart upon accumulation of wealth, and this passion may shut his eyes to the suffering caused by hunger, want and penury. His sole wish may be to accumulate maximum amount of wealth. Selfishness and indifference to tyranny and oppression are the result of certain incentives, which are mentioned in the Holy Quran and are discussed below.

Control Over the Incentives for Accumulation of Wealth

The Holy Quran states:[17]

---

[17] *Sūrah al-Ḥadīd*, 57:21, (publishers)

اِعْلَمُوٓا اَنَّمَا الْحَيٰوةُ الدُّنْيَا لَعِبٌ وَّلَهْوٌ وَّزِيْنَةٌ وَّتَفَاخُرٌۢ بَيْنَكُمْ وَتَكَاثُرٌ فِى الْاَمْوَالِ وَالْاَوْلَادِۭ ؕ كَمَثَلِ غَيْثٍ اَعْجَبَ الْكُفَّارَ نَبَاتُهٗ ثُمَّ يَهِيْجُ فَتَرٰىهُ مُصْفَرًّا ثُمَّ يَكُوْنُ حُطَامًا ؕ وَفِى الْاٰخِرَةِ عَذَابٌ شَدِيْدٌ ۙ وَّمَغْفِرَةٌ مِّنَ اللّٰهِ وَرِضْوَانٌ ؕ وَمَا الْحَيٰوةُ الدُّنْيَآ اِلَّا مَتَاعُ الْغُرُوْرِ ۟

[Know, that the life of this world is only a sport and a pass time, and an adornment, and a source of boastings, and of rivalry in multiplying riches. This life is like the vegetation produced whereby rejoices the tillers. Then it dries up and then it becomes broken pieces of straw. In the Hereafter, there is severe punishment and also forgiveness from Allah, and His pleasure. And the life of this world is nothing but temporary enjoyment of deceitful things.]

This verse outlines the core motivations that lie behind the human urge to amass wealth.

1. First motivation is the desire for entertainment, play, amusement and recreations like gambling, betting, horse racing, etc. Man seeks wealth so he can satisfy his desire for entertainment.
2. Second motivation is the desire for leisure, i.e. to have so much that there is no longer a need to work. People with this motivation want to be completely free all day to laze around and spend time playing cards, drinking wine etc.
3. Third motivation is the desire for elegance, i.e. to have the most luxurious clothes, dresses, cars and food.
4. Fourth motivation is the desire to be able to boast. Some people desire to be famous and be acknowledged in the

society as wealthy. I have observed that this obsession has so advanced in our country that people even take pride in acknowledging their subservience to those in power. For example, they would boast that, 'I pay such a huge amount in tax to the British government'. Thus, instead of feeling ashamed of being the subjects of a foreign power, they boast about the amount of tax they pay. Some happily boast: 'I am an orderly of such and such *Bara Ṣāḥib* (important person).'

5. Fifth motive is the mere addiction to accumulating wealth, i.e., when individuals start to compete with each other in accumulating greater wealth. If their neighbour has one million, they want 10 million, and if he has 10 million, they want 20 million.

As far as I have studied, these are the motivations for acquiring wealth that the Holy Quran has mentioned.

After describing these motivations, the Holy Quran says:[18]

$$...كَمَثَلِ غَيْثٍ اَعْجَبَ الْكُفَّارَ نَبَاتُهُ ثُمَّ يَهِيْجُ فَتَرٰىهُ مُصْفَرًّا ثُمَّ يَكُوْنُ حُطَامًا...$$

The Holy Quran likens the pursuit of wealth to a cloud in the sky that gives a farmer the hope that there would be rainfall, which would turn his fields green with new crops. But when it actually rains, it is either too much or too little. In both cases instead of

---

[18] *Ibid.* (publishers)

making a lot of money, the farmer witnesses the ruin of his crops because of too much or too little water.

The Quran then reminds us that not only is such wealth of little use in this world, it also leads to severe chastisement in the Hereafter for those who indulge in harmful occupations or pastimes. But those who restrain their base impulses are forgiven by God and are given the pleasure of His nearness.

The verses quoted above also contain a warning that a life given to worldly pursuits is no more than a mirage. We are thus cautioned against wasting our life in chasing fleeting and unreal shadows. We should not allow ourselves to be blinded by base passions; we must never lose sight of God's pleasure, which should always remain our supreme goal.

In these verses Allah the Almighty declares that all motivations that lead a man to the accumulation of wealth are unworthy and harmful, and likens them to a crop that withers away. In other words, just as a withered crop yields no benefit, so is the case with wealth accumulation. Therefore, a Muslim must avoid accumulating wealth under such compulsions, as they displease God. Since Allah is the source of all grace, the better course is to seek His grace and to overcome base desires.

It is clear that a person who follows the Islamic teachings would shun above motivations. Any wealth that he might accumulate would be devoted to noble causes that help to bridge the gulf between the rich and the poor, instead of widening it. Such a person has little reason to covet wealth for selfish ends. A man's desire to earn money arises out of basically three impulses.

1. To meet his own legitimate needs;
2. Beyond meeting the personal needs, he might desire money with a view to helping mankind and earning God's pleasure; or
3. He might seek money to fulfil vain desires described above i.e., personal pleasure, self-indulgence, pride or plain greed.

It goes without saying that only persons driven by the third impulse would stoop to unfair and foul means, and would exploit others. This situation would be avoided if the first two reasons for earning money were dominant. Anyone who earns just enough to satisfy his own needs or who spends the excess wealth for helping others and other good deeds would not hurt other Individuals or his nation in general.

Improper Use of Wealth Forbidden

I proceed now to elaborate on how Islam forbids the improper use of wealth. In regard to the true Muslims, the Holy Quran says:[19]

...عَنِ اللَّغْوِ مُعْرِضُونَ ۞

That is: Muslims are those who stay away from frivolous acts.

They stay away from pursuits or activities that are of little benefit, such as, playing chess, cards or other games wasteful of time. Islam

---

[19] *Sūrah al-Mu'minūn*, 23:4, (publishers)

directs all believers to desist from all such useless (*laghw*) pursuits. Accordingly, idleness, gossiping among friends or other useless activities are not approved in Islam. Indolent life style is also regarded as *laghw*.

Consider the case of a son who inherits considerable wealth from his father, but then spends his entire day with friends in idle gossip. His friends drop in for friendly chats. They come and go, flattering him with all manner of titles, and this continues all day. Such 'friends' are always there to entice him into other evil ways, involving women, gambling, alcohol and other extravagances. And the heir, of course, entertains them, offering tea with things to eat or sumptuous dinners, depending on the size of his wealth. However, these people are fed not because they are poor or need help, but because this is just a way of whiling away the time. Islam strictly prohibits such forms of recreation, and Muslims are admonished to stay away from pursuits that yield nothing worthwhile.

A man who lives off the income or inheritance of his parents and does not engage himself in useful work must weigh what benefit he or his country is deriving from his idleness. Certainly, his idle existence does no good to anyone—himself, his nation, or the world at large.

Islam enjoins such a person to not waste his time, but rather put his resources in the service of humanity and not allow his personal capabilities to go waste. If he has no need to work for a living, he might volunteer himself to help humanity, his country or his religion. He can thereby avoid wasting his time and, by spending time beneficially, he can turn into a useful member of society.

In short, Islam forbids activities that waste time and do not contribute to the betterment of one's life. It is for this reason that the

Holy Prophet[sa] asked men not to wear jewellery or silk. Similarly, he forbade the use of utensils made of gold or silver. Jewellery is not totally forbidden for women, but the Holy Prophet[sa] disliked its use in everyday life. While jewellery may help to embellish women's beauty, Islam disapproves of excessive expenditures on it, as it might hinder economic progress of society, make them arrogant, or give rise to rivalries that feed on greed and avarice. Thus, women may use jewellery within certain limits; but men are totally barred.

The above comments also apply to articles that the rich keep for show and display, but which serve no purpose. Some people spend large sums of money on antique China and think that they have made a good investment. Old carpets and old China command exorbitant prices and many Europeans buy them not because they are of some use but because they are rare and a source of pride for the owner. Their prices are high only because of the antique value; otherwise, similar carpets or china can be purchased for a fraction of the price. Islam declares all such expenditures to be *laghw*—which provide no real benefit and are meant only for ostentation. The Holy Prophet[sa] by his own practice disapproved of such indulgences and admonished the believers not to waste time and money in pursuit of vain desires.

Cinema and theatre are another area of waste in this day and age. I once made a rough calculation and was astonished to discover the enormous amount the public spends on this pastime. In Lahore, I hear, there are some 25 cinema houses, each of which nets in about three thousand rupees [Rs.] a week. If one assumes the average weekly profit to be Rs. 2,500 per cinema, or Rs. 10,000 monthly, the annual revenue of an average cinema would come to Rs. 120,000. If we assume there are only twenty cinemas in Lahore, their total profit just in Lahore would come to some Rs. 2,400,000. If the whole of India was assumed to have fifty times the number of cinemas in Lahore (although it is likely to be more), there would be over a thousand cinemas in India, yielding a staggering sum of Rs.120 million annually. This expenditure does not include the substantial sums spent by cinemagoers on refreshments and related entertainment, which, in itself, could amount to a similar figure. In other words, cinema and related expenditures could account for some 250 million rupees every year, which equals one-fourth of the entire revenue of the Government of India. Thus a sum equal to one-fourth of what the entire government spends in India is spent on cinema—an activity that does not materially lead to any benefit either for the country or for cinema-goers.

The Holy Quran shuts the doors of all such avenues of wastage, and holds true believers to be those who stay away from such frivolous activities and do not spend a penny of their income on them. The European countries with democratic governments are eager to promote their economic progress but spend a fortune building cinema houses and theatres. In fact, it is quite likely that England would find the existing number of cinemas inadequate and would greatly increase their numbers after the war [World War II]. They would want everyone who is deprived of this luxury to partake of it and spend their time and money in cinemas. However, Islam categorically rejects all such activities that are not in the interest of mankind at large. If these teachings of Islam were adopted, the society would become largely egalitarian, as a big incentive to earn illicit wealth is the urge to satisfy vain desires.

Extravagance Forbidden

Secondly, Islam forbids extravagance, i.e., excessive spending on things or activities that are acceptable within their due limits. An example of extravagance is the construction of tall structures or expensive decorative gardens for just ostentation. There are, of course, orchards with fruit trees, which are not forbidden in Islam. However, some large private gardens are made only for display and personal enjoyment and pleasure. This was so when kings built huge gardens just to entertain themselves with song and dance. Spending large amounts of money for personal leisure is considered extravagance.

However, large gardens for public use, as are found in many cities, where people can go for enjoyment, relaxation and exercise is not banned in Islam at all. If a city spends a large sum of money on a garden for its inhabitants to enjoy, that is a legitimate expense.

To illustrate, Lahore currently has a population of about 900,000. If Lahore Corporation were to lay out public gardens and parks at the cost of a few hundred thousand rupees, Islam would not call it extravagance, as the whole town would derive benefit from these gardens. The per capita expenditure on such a garden would be quite reasonable relative to the benefits that the entire population would receive. On the other hand, if a king or a rich person were to lay out similar gardens for the sole use of his family, Islam would disapprove of it. Such expenditure would mean that millions have been spent for the benefit of a few individuals only, while the same expenditure could have benefited hundreds of thousands of people, which might have also been beneficial for their health.

Thus Islam does not stop us from spending money on people's genuine needs. It only restricts individuals from wasteful expenditures that come about by neglecting the rights of public at-large. If a multi-story building is built with hundreds of offices for the use of thousands of people, it is a legitimate expense. However, if an individual builds a house with large number of rooms to show off his wealth, then that expenditure would be considered extravagant and not legitimate in Islam. Such a person would be answerable before God on the day of judgement to explain why he did not spend money for the benefit of mankind?

The example of the Taj Mahal is close to home. This fine mausoleum is renowned all over the world, attracting admirers from far and wide. I myself have visited it a number of times, and it is undoubtedly a marvellous structure, exquisite in form, grace and beauty. But it is in fact no more than a personal monument built by an emperor to immortalise his love for his queen. From the Islamic point of view, the enormous amount of money spent on it was not well spent. If the same money had been spent for the betterment of the poor, the downtrodden and the orphans, hundreds of thousands of people could have benefitted for a long time to come. It would have been a better use of wealth if such people could have been provided resources for food, clothing and shelter.

There is no doubt that from a technical and engineering perspective, the Taj Mahal is a work of art. We all appreciate it and like to visit it. However, the reality is that we must also recognise that such magnificent buildings, which are built for the benefit of a few individuals alone, are not permitted in Islam. On the other hand, the buildings built for the benefit of public at large, no matter how tall and big, are not against Islamic teachings. It is the expenditure on things beyond one's reasonable needs that is forbidden. Example of expenditures forbidden in the Holy Quran and hadith are: big buildings, large expenses on gardens to display wealth, over-indulgence in food and extravagance in the purchase of clothes, cars, horses, furniture, etc. By limiting the scope of what one might spend on, Islam limits the need for accumulating wealth.

Spending Money to Gain Political Power Forbidden

Islam similarly forbids passing on political power to individuals solely because of their wealth. I have already spoken about the Quranic injunction: 'to make over the trusts to those entitled to them', meaning that we should only accord authority to those who are best able to hold office regardless of their economic status. Thus, Islam reproves accumulation of wealth in order to gain political power or high office. It instructs Muslims to elect people solely on the basis of merit and not to be swayed by wealth and high social or economic status.

Greed for Wealth Accumulation Curbed

Then there are people who accumulate wealth for its own sake. Islam disapproves of this tendency too. As stated in the Quran:[20]

---

[20] *Sūrah at-Taubah*, 9:34–35, (publishers)

> ...وَالَّذِينَ يَكْنِزُونَ الذَّهَبَ وَالْفِضَّةَ وَلَا يُنْفِقُونَهَا فِى سَبِيلِ اللهِ فَبَشِّرْهُمْ بِعَذَابٍ أَلِيمٍ ۞ يَوْمَ يُحْمَى عَلَيْهَا فِى نَارِ جَهَنَّمَ فَتُكْوَىٰ بِهَا جِبَاهُهُمْ وَجُنُوبُهُمْ وَظُهُورُهُمْ هَٰذَا مَا كَنَزْتُمْ لِأَنْفُسِكُمْ فَذُوقُوا مَا كُنْتُمْ تَكْنِزُونَ ۞

That is: Those who hoard up gold and silver and do not spend it in the way of Allah, are given the tidings of a painful punishment. On the day when that gold and silver shall be heated in the fire of Hell, and their foreheads and their sides and their backs shall be branded therewith and it shall be said to them, this is what you treasured up for yourselves and for the benefit of your families, and had deprived the general public of their benefit...

The last part of the verse, ...فَذُوقُوا مَا كُنْتُمْ تَكْنِزُونَ ۞ 'so now taste what you used to treasure up' refers to the gold and silver that did not give any benefit to the general public. God says that on the day of judgement this gold and silver is returned to you. But since gold and silver are of no use in the afterlife, it only 'brands their foreheads and their sides and their backs'. In this way they find out how sinful it was to withhold wealth from the benefit of mankind.

Although this example does not literally relate to the misuse of wealth, withholding of wealth is akin to misusing it since that prevents wealth from benefitting mankind at large. In effect, therefore, hoarding or misusing wealth amount to the same thing, i.e., denying its use for productive purposes.

Islam categorically rejects all motives that lead to excessive hoarding of wealth. Since the foundation of every action is its motive, no Muslim can accumulate so much wealth that it becomes a hindrance for human development. For example, some people spend millions on the upkeep of race horses and gambling. However, according to Islamic teachings, a Muslim may keep a horse for riding, but not for racing.

Because Islam rejects all such motives, it also eliminates the need to accumulate excessive wealth. The urge to make more and more money comes about when one tries to emulate others who have enriched themselves or who spend huge amounts on extravagances such as horse racing, or when one seeks to accumulate wealth for their own sake. Since Islam demands of us that we curb all such temptations, the urge to earn beyond a reasonable amount dies away.

Further Steps to Control Those of Weaker Nature

The teachings that I have expounded above are by way of exhortations. However, mere sermon or admonition may not stop people with weaker dispositions from accumulating wealth beyond prescribed limits. Thus, the Islamic shariah—whose implementation is the government's responsibility—contains specific provisions against wealth accumulation beyond its proper limits. These provisions are listed below.

Barriers to Illegitimate Accumulation of Wealth in Islam

Prohibition of Interest (*Ribā*)

Islam forbids lending and borrowing of money on interest, which also entails certain limits on commerce. It is ironic that this country's intellectuals tend to look with favour on Communism, and yet are inclined to support an economic order based on interest. The fact of the matter is that interest has been the most important cause of economic and financial catastrophes in the world.

Interest enables a shrewd and clever businessman to accumulate vast amounts of money, which then enables him to control markets or establish large factories, thereby reducing many people to perpetual economic subservience. If one were to examine the list of the world's richest men, it would be found that it was made up of mostly people who owe their rise to interest. They start with a small amount of capital but soon establish a reputation of creditworthiness, which allows them to leverage their small personal capital many times over via bank borrowing and overdrafts, thereby becoming super-rich in just a few years. There are others, who may not have any significant amount to invest, but use their wit and contacts to cultivate relationship with bank managers to borrow large sums of money. Only a tiny percentage of the rich make their entire money from personal capital.

Interest is one of the most destructive economic forces in the world and a major hurdle that stops the poor from moving forward. It is thus imperative that mankind rid itself of interest. If the rich were unable to borrow money on interest, they would be left with one of the two choices. They could expand their business by including more people in their partnership, which would of necessity involve spreading the earnings over a wider group of people. Or, alternatively, they would not be able to grow their business and become a hindrance to other small businesses. Either way, there would be a more equitable distribution of wealth. It would also prevent the accumulation of wealth into the hands of a few people, which is extremely dangerous and detrimental for overall economic progress.

Unfortunately despite the clearly visible harmful effects of interest, people remain entangled in the deadly web of interest, and do not ponder over the destructive impact that this financial system has at national and international levels. Ironically, even the supporters of Communism do not escape from this trap, for they do not find anything wrong with interest even though it is the root of capitalism. There are communists around the world who do not see anything wrong with interest, and as such end up inadvertently lending support to the very foundation of capitalism.

Islam adopts a rather broader definition of interest. According to the Islamic definition, certain transactions, which are generally not considered to fall within its purview, nevertheless fall within its domain and are therefore prohibited. Islam defines interest as any transaction where the profit is guaranteed. Therefore all trusts, [local monopolistic arrangements] which are set up to guarantee profit by destroying competition, are to be considered un-Islamic. For example, suppose fifteen or twenty large businesses in a country got together and formed a monopoly that fixed prices and restricted competition. Then a commodity that sells for (say) two rupees in a competitive market could sell at an artificial monopolistic price of (say) five rupees. Since everyone would be colluding to sell the commodity at five rupees, consumers would not be able to shop around for the best price and would have no choice but to pay the higher price.

Smaller businesses would not have the ability to compete with such trusts. Even if they tried to compete by reducing the price, the trust with its monopolistic power would start a price war, which they would find impossible to win. Thus, all monopolistic arrangements are dangerous both for the country and for the global economy.

In connection with certain commercial schemes of Ahmadiyya Muslim Community, I once had the occasion to collect information concerning the shellac business, which requires only a small capital to set up and is confined to certain areas of India, notably the Patiala state. I was surprised to discover that one single European firm had established a monopoly over its trade. On enquiring as to how this monopoly had emerged, I learned that other firms were very small, while this firm was doing business of far greater magnitude. It not only controlled the shellac trade, but was also engaged in trading wheat, cloth, jute and other products. If any business ventured to compete, the European firm would reduce the shellac price so low that a new entrant could not survive for long. In fact the new entrant was often made to sell its remaining inventory to the European firm, which would then recoup its lost earnings by raising the shellac price. That is how the firm managed to maintain its monopoly power and did not allow a competitor to come in. It is as such evident that all monopolistic arrangements that seek guaranteed profit hurt public at large, and are therefore against the Islamic precepts.

Similarly, cartels formed across countries are also unlawful under the Islamic economic system. Such cartels involve businesses belonging to different countries, which get together and agree on a price for a particular commodity. While trusts are monopolistic arrangements between local businesses, cartels are formed across countries. For example, firms from America and England, or America, England and Germany, or England and India might come together to agree on the terms for trading in specific commodities. Suppose these firms entered into an agreement in the chemicals industry, which is largely in the hands of American, English and German firms. If firms from these countries were to collude in fixing the prices of medicines, the world would be compelled to pay the higher prices, and deliver the negotiated profits to the cartel network.

The system of cartels is so dangerous that many governments are troubled by it. Just a few days ago the government prosecuted some businesses on anti-trust charges and even punished them. Islam is against any mechanism that leads to guaranteed profit and hence the monopolization of wealth in a few hands. It seeks to ensure that money continues to circulate throughout the economy so that the poorer segment of society also has a chance to improve itself. Thus, cartels and monopolies are not allowed in an Islamic system of governance.

Withholding Supplies from the Market Forbidden

Islam also demands that supplies should not be deliberately withheld from the market with the purpose of artificially boosting prices. If a person hoards goods for this reason, he does so by going against the Islamic principles. If a trader has wheat but deliberately withholds its supply from the public in order to raise prices, he is engaged in a sinful activity, according to Islamic teachings.

Some people believe that regulation of markets by the state is a modern economic concept, but Islam has always recognized its need. The British have now come to recognize that hoarding with the purpose of extracting higher prices is not good for the economy, but Islam recognized it thirteen centuries ago. An Islamic government would require that no trader could hoard his goods, and if any trader were found to be doing so, the government would be entitled to force liquidation of his inventory at appropriate market prices. Thus, the broader Islamic principle mandates that any good that is a need of the people must not be artificially hoarded. The word used for hoarding is *iḥtikār* which primarily refers to the hoarding of food grains. But in line with the Islamic rules of jurisprudence, this injunction would be interpreted broadly to cover all goods that are withheld from the market with the intent of raising the price.

Injunction Against Artificial Lowering of Prices

Similarly, Islam does not permit that prices be forced down by artificial means, because, as mentioned above, this too enables unscrupulous traders to strangle their rivals by forcing them to sell at reduced prices.

During his reign, Haḍrat Umar[ra], while inspecting the market, came across a trader from outside Madinah who was selling dried grapes at prices that local producers and traders could not compete against. Ḥaḍrat Umar[ra] ordered the man to remove his produce from the market or to sell it at the price prevailing in Madinah. When asked for the reasons of this order, Ḥaḍrat Umar[ra] replied that without such an order the local merchants would have suffered a loss even though they were not charging an undue price.

It is true that some companions questioned the validity of this order in view of the saying of the Holy Prophet[sa] that market prices should not be interfered with. However, their objection was not well founded, since the prohibition against state intervention in market prices by the Holy Prophet[sa] pertained to interference with the free interplay of supply and demand. The government should avoid undue interference, as it would provide no benefit to consumers while inflicting serious losses upon traders.

The validity of this principle is borne out by recent events. The government failed in its attempt to fix the wheat price because, in the prevailing war conditions, no trader was able to sell at cost price and remain in business. The result was that the normal market activity for wheat came to a standstill and a black market emerged. Starving people were ready to buy wheat at whatever price they could afford. The price that was fixed at six rupees a 'maund'[21] by the government at once soared to sixteen rupees in the black market. People did not even report to the government about the black market because their survival depended on it. Several months ago, I had drawn the government's attention to this danger but this warning went unheeded. The right course was adopted only after a great deal of suffering and serious unrest among the public. The

---

[21] A measure of weight used in India, equal to about 82 pounds. (publishers)

earlier wheat price control order was meant to safeguard farmers' interests, but in reality the farmers lost heavily while the traders netted large profits.

In short, the Holy Prophet[sa] prohibited only improper interference with price levels or unnecessary disruption in the normal operation of supply and demand. He did not forbid regulation to check abnormal price movements whether prices are driven artificially high or artificially low. The prohibition of *iḥtikār*, which is firmly established according to the sayings of the Holy Prophet[sa], also bears this out, because *iḥtikār* only means that artificial increases in prices be checked. Therefore, Ḥaḍrat Umar's[ra] action, although an interference in the market, was a necessary regulation; it was consistent with shariah and demonstrated a sound principle of Islamic teachings.

The aforementioned are the three sources of unlawful wealth accumulation that Islam has prohibited. In this manner, Islam blocks all channels that lead to the unlawful and excessive accumulation of wealth.

Since clever and shrewd people might still find ways to accumulate excessive wealth, to the detriment of the less fortunate, Islam has adopted the following means to address this problem.

Measures Adopted in Shariah to Achieve a Just Economic System

Zakat

Islam introduced the system of zakat, which is a 2.5% annual tax on wealth that is held in the form of gold, silver, currency or other assets for a period of more than a year. The proceeds of this tax are used to promote welfare of the poor. Thus, if a person has forty rupees in his possession and he keeps the money for the entire year, he must pay one rupee as zakat to the government.

It should be noted that this is not an income tax on earnings. Instead, zakat is payable on accumulated wealth and is spent for the welfare of the poor. zakat is due on all kinds of wealth, whether coins, animals, produce, jewellery or other tradable assets. However, jewellery that women use normally, and especially if they also occasionally share it with less fortunate women, is exempt from zakat. According to Islamic scholars, if jewellery is used only for personal use and is not shared with poor women, zakat should preferably be paid for it. In any event, Islam strictly mandates that zakat be paid on those pieces of jewellery that are not in common use.

Zakat is payable every year as long as the wealth in one's possession does not fall below the taxable minimum. Zakat is paid not only on capital but also on the accumulated profit that it fetches. The moral basis of zakat is that if anyone, despite all the provisions against excessive accumulation of wealth, still manages to accumulate money, the Islamic government will tax a portion of it every year, on grounds that, because of their hard work, the poor have a right and a share in the wealth accumulated by the rich. Therefore, a system has been put in place to take away the due right of the poor from the rich every year.

Khumus—One-Fifth Royalty on Mining

A second means for accumulating undue wealth is through the exploitation of mines. Islam deals with this issue by giving the state the right to impose a royalty of one-fifth of the produce of the mine. This fifth is due on any income derived from the mine. Any excess income saved by the owners of the mine for over a year will be separately subject to zakat year after year. In this way, the government has a direct ownership stake in the mines. It also has a share in the money saved from excess income of the mines, which it collects for the benefit of the poor.

Voluntary Charity

Islam also enjoins individuals to offer voluntary charity. It is prescribed for every person and is to be given to orphans and the poor and for the care and support of the weak. This emphasis on charity also helps to redistribute the wealth so that it does not excessively accumulate in the hands of a few.

Islamic Law of Inheritance

If despite the above safeguards an individual still manages to leave behind money or property after his death, it would be redistributed among his family members immediately after his death according to the Islamic law of inheritance. Islam does not allow anyone to leave his estate to any single heir, but instead his property must be distributed to all legal heirs. All sons and daughters are given a legal share, as well as parents, wife, and husband, and, in certain instances, even brothers and sisters. The Holy Quran clearly states that no one is allowed to deviate from these rules and pass on his property to a single heir. Islamic law forcefully distributes a person's property after his death to all legal heirs, and every relative must be given the share prescribed in the Holy Quran.

It is surprising that while people favour interest, which causes great financial inequity in the world, they are against the enforced distribution of the wealth of a deceased among all legal heirs. Instead, they allow a single son to inherit the entire estate, thereby causing wealth to remain perpetually concentrated in a single family.

However, in the Islamic system no matter how wealthy a person, his wealth will be redistributed, generation after generation until his progeny is at the same level as the average person. In this way no matter how large an estate or how vast a person's wealth, it cannot last more than a few generations. After this time, the succeeding generations would feel the need for generating their own wealth.

The reason for the concentration of wealth in the hands of a few rich people in Europe and the United States is that, under the British law, the eldest son can inherit the entire property, and in the United States, a person may pass on his entire wealth to just a single son. Thus, other children, parents, brothers and sisters, or the spouse may be left with nothing.

Sometimes the super-rich bequeath a large part of their inheritance to the eldest son to preserve family legacies and leave only meagre amounts to other relatives. Islam considers this practice entirely wrong and maintains the welfare of the entire society to be the paramount consideration. No matter how high and noble a family might consider itself to be, Islam wants large estates to be divided and further subdivided over generations so that the poor do not have to compete with large capital owners who prevent the poor from making economic progress.

Thus, in the first place, Islam curbs the inducements and impulses that result in accumulating excessive wealth. Secondly, it forbids spending of money on fulfilling one's vain desires and other wasteful pursuits. Thirdly, it disallows all such avenues of generating wealth that provide guaranteed profit. Fourthly, it stipulates the payment of zakat and voluntary charity. If despite all these mechanisms, someone is able to accumulate excessive wealth due to his wit and astuteness, and there is a danger that his wealth might hinder the progress of the underprivileged, Islam stipulates that his wealth be distributed among the heirs immediately after his demise.

Thus if a person has ten million rupees and has ten sons, his wealth would be equally divided into one million for each son and then if they each have ten sons the wealth would get further divided into one hundred thousand rupees in the following generation. By the time of the third generation, only ten thousand rupees would be left for a family. This way, even a large estate would get greatly diminished within three or four generations and it would not become a hurdle in the progress of the poor. The disposition of wealth after one's demise can only be prevented for that part of the property that is given away for the good of the public to a non-profit organization. Obviously, anyone who accumulates capital with a view to supporting the welfare of the poor and the public at large cannot be expected to use unlawful means to earn money.

The Islamic economic system is thus naturally furnished with pruning devices that come into action if someone starts to have excessive amounts of wealth. The excess capital starts to go to the government, or is distributed among other people, or gets distributed among the descendents. Under this system, no one can remain rich forever and no family can maintain its financial dominance generation after generation or be able to subjugate the poorer sections of the society.

It is regrettable that Muslims have not fully followed Islamic guidance on this matter. The teaching about zakat is there but it is ignored. Extravagance is prohibited but they continue to indulge in it. The laws of inheritance are not strictly followed. Nevertheless, there is some partial observance, and consequently, the gap between the rich and poor is less extreme in Islamic countries than in other.

It is still possible that the above-mentioned Islamic injunctions would not fully address the problem of economic inequity. In particular, it is possible that the money that the government collects is diverted back to the rich upper class in various ways. The Holy Quran also addresses this issue and restricts the ways in which government revenue can be spent.

Responsibilities of the Government

Curb on Spending in Favour of the Rich

Allah the Almighty directs in the Holy Quran:[22]

$$\text{مَا أَفَاءَ اللّٰهُ عَلٰى رَسُولِهٖ مِنْ أَهْلِ الْقُرٰى فَلِلّٰهِ وَ لِلرَّسُولِ وَلِذِى الْقُرْبٰى وَالْيَتٰمٰى وَالْمَسٰكِيْنِ وَابْنِ السَّبِيْلِ ۙ كَيْ لَا يَكُوْنَ دُوْلَةً ۢ بَيْنَ الْأَغْنِيَاءِ مِنْكُمْ ؕ وَمَا اٰتٰكُمُ الرَّسُوْلُ فَخُذُوْهُ ۚ وَمَا نَهٰكُمْ عَنْهُ فَانْتَهُوْا ۚ وَاتَّقُوا اللّٰهَ ؕ إِنَّ اللّٰهَ شَدِيْدُ الْعِقَابِ}$$

Meaning that: Whatever Allah has given to His Messenger as spoils from towns, is for Allah and for the Messenger, and for the near of kin and the orphans and the needy and the wayfarers who are travelling to convey the Word of God. These commandments have been given to ensure that the wealth may not circulate only among those of you who are rich.

These verses illustrate how God has protected the rights of the poor, and thereby greatly strengthened the foundations of the Islamic economic order and ensured that the economic condition does not worsen. If the economic system had been left alone and the rights of different parties had not been specified, all money would have accumulated in a few hands and the poor would have continued to suffer in deprivation. The Quran, therefore, mandates that the money the government collects

---

[22] *Sūrah al-Ḥashr*, 59:8, (publishers)

must not return to the rich, but instead be used for uplifting the less privileged sections of society.

The share allotted in this verse to Allah and His Apostle is, in fact, also a share intended for the poor. The names of God and His Prophet[sa] are used because at times the state is called upon to build places of worship, schools, and hospitals. If the rights of only the poor had been mentioned, some might have objected to government spending on places of worship, hospitals, roads or schools. By specifically mentioning the names of God and his Prophet[sa], any grounds for misunderstanding have been removed. It goes without saying that Allah's share in reality is also for the poor since God does not need any money and similarly Prophet's share belongs to the poor as the Prophet[sa] is a mortal who would one day leave this world. Mention of the Prophet[sa] by name here implies that the reference is to the system he put in place.

The expression *dhil-qurbā* [near of kin] occurring in these verses is sometimes incorrectly held to imply that the family of the Holy Prophet[sa] have a right in government revenue. However, the Holy Prophet[sa] has categorically declared that his descendants are not permitted to accept charity or a share of the zakat. Thus, the Quranic expression does not refer to blood relatives of the Holy Prophet[sa], but signifies those people who are exclusively engaged day and night in the devotion and worship of God and thus become part of the family of Allah and His Prophet. The expression *dhil-qurbā* is intended to imply that those devoted to the service of religion should not be considered worthless people, for by striving for the nearness of Allah and by facilitating the attainment of His nearness for others, they are entitled to the resources from public funds.

People who are engaged in teaching the Holy Quran and Hadith, or are working for the propagation of faith, will not be able to make a living, and are, according to this verse, entitled to have a share in these revenues. If the government did not provide them with the necessary funds, it would result in either their moral standard suffering because of the strain of constant want, forcing them to beg; or they would be forced to give up the service of religion in order to earn their livelihood. The Holy Quran contains an express injunction that among the Muslims there should always be people dedicated to the service of religion for all hours of the day and night.

Therefore, *dhil-qurbā* refers to people dedicated to the service of religion and according to Islam this class of people has a definite claim on the State's resources.

To emphasise further that essential point is reiterated in the concluding portion of the passage. 'Accept what the Prophet allows you but desist from claiming that which he has forbidden.' The rich should not try to get back the wealth taken from them by Islam in the interest of the poor, for this was essential for the peace and prosperity of society.

State Obligated to Provide for Primary Needs of All

The Islamic State, on gaining the resources, implemented the above outlined precepts and assumed responsibility for meeting each person's needs for food and clothing. In the time of Ḥaḍrat Umar[ra], when the New Order was completely established, a census was taken, involving registration of the individual's name, in order to facilitate the task of providing food and clothing to everyone. Even European writers acknowledge that it was Ḥaḍrat Umar[ra] who first held census and initiated the system of registration. In order to carry out the responsibility of providing food and clothing to everyone, the government needed to know the number people living in the country. It is generally believed today that the Soviet State was the first to recognise its responsibilities towards its people in meeting their primary needs, but the fact is that Islam had done this more than thirteen hundred years ago. Registers maintained by Ḥaḍrat Umar's[ra] administration were thorough and complete. They listed the members in each family, their ages, needs, and the quantity and kind of food sanctioned.

It is recorded in history that Ḥaḍrat Umar[ra] in his earlier decisions had not provided for the needs of suckling babies because an infant's due ration was granted only after it had been weaned. One night, while out on a round of quiet inspection, Ḥaḍrat Umar[ra] heard the wailing sound of an infant, which made him pause. But the cries continued, even though the mother tried to put the child to sleep by patting him. At last Ḥaḍrat Umar[ra] entered the tent and enquired of the mother: 'Why do you not suckle the child?' The woman did not recognise the Khalīfah and answered, 'Ḥaḍrat Umar[ra] has decreed that no ration be granted in the case of infants until they were weaned. We are poor people with hardly enough to make both ends meet. I have weaned the child early so that we should get a measure of ration that includes the child'. Ḥaḍrat Umar[ra] was shocked when he heard this, and he hastened at once to the *Baitul-Māl* (Public Treasury) muttering painfully to himself, 'You have weakened the coming generation of the Arabs by causing infants to be prematurely weaned; the responsibility for this lies on your head.' He opened the door of the store and lifted a sack of flour on his own back. When an attendant offered to carry it for him, he replied, 'No. I failed to discharge my responsibility. I must make amends for it myself.' He then carried the flour to the woman and ordered the next day that a ration be granted for a child from the day it was born, because the nursing mother, in any case, needed better nourishment.

It is therefore beyond dispute that as soon as Islam was in a position to do so, it put into operation a fair and just economic system. In fact, it is evident from the Holy Quran that this system originated at the dawn of history, in the time of Ḥaḍrat Adam[as], not with Ḥaḍrat Umar[ra]. In the earliest revelation to Ḥaḍrat Adam[as] we find him directed by God to live in a garden wherein it was ordained that:[23]

اِنَّ لَكَ اَلَّا تَجُوْعَ فِيْهَا وَلَا تَعْرٰى ۞ وَاَنَّكَ لَا تَظْمَؤُا فِيْهَا وَلَا تَضْحٰى ۞

Meaning that: 'O Adam, We have ordained for you to live in the garden and it is provided for you that you will not hunger therein, nor will you be naked; and you will not thirst therein, nor will you be exposed to the sun.'

It is a mistake to assume, as many people do, that this garden was not located on this earth and that only when he entered paradise in the Hereafter, would man be free from want as depicted in this passage. The Holy Quran is clear on the point that Ḥaḍrat Adam[as] was raised as a Prophet in this world, as is

---

[23] *Sūrah Ṭā Hā*, 20:119–120, (publishers)

said: 'I am about to place a vicegerent in the earth'. (*Sūrah al-Baqarah*, 2:31). And a person born in this world is undoubtedly exposed to hunger and thirst, and is in need of clothing and shelter. This verse therefore clearly means that Ḥaḍrat Adam[as] was given the Law for the creation of a civilised society and its implementation was intended to ensure fulfilment of just needs of its members on the basis of a system of joint responsibility of all. Food, clothing and shelter were laid down as the primary needs; and the new society was made responsible for ensuring that all its members were properly provided for in these respects.

This was the first revelation and the earliest dawn of civilisation established through Ḥaḍrat Adam[as]; and from the very outset Almighty God made it manifestly clear that He is indeed God not only of the strong and well-fed, but of all high and low, rich and poor. He never willed that a portion of humanity should wallow in luxury while the rest suffer from want of food and clothing.

This was the Order that Islam came to re-establish. Unfortunately the system was in operation only for a brief period, but this is not unusual. Great upward movements in human progress are followed by decline as old customs and practices reassert themselves. Nevertheless, the achieved progress is not forgotten but remains in the people's collective memory, and noble and fair-minded persons continue to strive to re-institute the earlier improvements. Thus, although the earlier Islamic Order disappeared, it is now the Ahmadiyya Muslim Community that seeks to re-establish it in the world. This Community, when it gets the opportunity, would seek to prevent undue accumulation of wealth in the hands of a few, while striving to improve the lot of the poor and ensuring that everyone gets the basic requirements of food, clothing and shelter.

To sum up, the Islamic economic system is based on:

1. Exhortation against undue accumulation of wealth;
2. Curbing the motivation behind undue accumulation of wealth;
3. Insistence on expeditious redistribution of concentrated wealth; and
4. Recognition that it is the State's responsibility to spend money on meeting the legitimate basic needs of the poor and weak members of society.

It is only the Islamic system that is complete, comprehensive and satisfactory because:

- It allows individuals to provide for the life Hereafter;
- It fosters in man the habits of plain, simple and productive living;
- It is not based on force and compulsion;
- It does not crush individual capabilities;
- It provides for the comfort and progress of the poor and the weak, and
- It removes the basis for the rise of opposition and enmity.

Communism

Communism is an economic system that provides a sharp contrast to the economic system discussed above. Because it has become prominent in discussions, I would like to make a few observations about this system.

Communism claims that:

1. Everyone must work to the best of their capacity;
2. Everyone must be provided with income sufficient to meet the normal needs.
3. The remaining surplus belongs to the State as a trustee for the people.

These principles are based on the notion that there should be equality among all people. As long as a person worked to the best of his capacity, he was entitled to payment on the same scale as all others, who, too, worked up to their capacity. Thus no one was entitled to possess wealth in excess of others; any excess wealth would be appropriated by the State.

This is the economic side of Communism. But this viewpoint has also a political dimension, which falls outside the scope of my discussion for today. I would therefore not touch it.

As far as the basic principle is concerned, it is entirely correct that all must be properly fed, clothed, and housed; all must have access to facilities for education and health. In brief, the basic needs of all should be fulfilled. On this point Islam is fully in accord with Communism. But there is a fundamental difference. While Islam leaves the door open for individual enterprise and due development of individual capabilities, Communism shuts that door completely.

Fundamental Difference Between Islam and Communism

In fact individual freedom is indispensable not only for the proper development of human capacities, but also to allow individuals to freely choose their actions so that they can provide for the life to come. Communism blocks the avenues of individual initiative and destroys personal freedom of choice. And, that is a major flaw of that system. Thus, Islam and Communism share common objectives with respect to meeting basic needs of everyone, but differ with respect to the means adopted to achieve that end.

Undoubtedly, Russia has made remarkable economic progress with the programme it chalked out under the influence of the Communist philosophy. The general public, at least in European Russia has become materially better off than before. (Communist leaders might dispute that the progress is confined only to the European part). We have to admit that the poor people in Russia are better fed, better clad, better housed and provided with better facilities for education and medical relief. Thus, as far as these achievements are concerned, they are very much in accord with the Islamic spirit of fairness in economic treatment. But as noted, Islam does not approve of the means adopted by the Communist Party to achieve this.

Objections Against Communism on the Basis of Religion

As I represent the Islamic point of view, I take up first those aspects of the Communist economic system that bear on religion.

1. No Scope of Voluntary Efforts

My foremost objection against Communism—an objection which all beliefs in life after death must have—is that it leaves little scope for individual voluntary effort, which alone is the basis for earning merit for the life to come. Instead of withholding some reasonable portion of his wealth for the State, and leaving the individual free to spend the rest as he wishes, a person is left with nothing more than what suffices for his needs. This deprives him of the means to provide for the life to come. He is given food, he can clothe himself, he is assured of shelter, his education and medical care, but he has not a penny left to provide for the life Hereafter. In other words, Communism looks after only the material side of a person's life—which may span forty to fifty years—but entirely ignores the life Hereafter that is believed to be everlasting.

This is something to which no one who is convinced of the truth of religion and wishes to follow its teachings could ever be reconciled. Islam, for instance, expects, as some other religions do, that its followers spread out and carry its message to the world's four corners so that mankind can seek deliverance. Anyone who remained away from Islam would miss this deliverance, and on the day of judgement he would face God as a guilty person. You may call a Muslim mad or a fool for holding such beliefs, but as far as he is concerned and as long as his convictions remain what they are, missionary activity devolves upon him as a duty that he may not shirk in any circumstances. After all, if he wished well for mankind, he would feel obliged to deliver the message that he believes is for its benefit. No one would like his friend to fall in a ditch or be shot to death. How, then, can one reconcile himself to his friends being given the everlasting punishment and be deprived of Paradise and God's nearness and pleasure. Call it what you like, for a person attached to his religion, it is a strong desire to help his brother improve his moral and practical life. There is no room for this sort of work under Communism; any such efforts would be politically curbed.

I speak on this point from actual experience of conditions prevailing in Soviet Russia. Some time back, I had sent an Ahmadiyya Missionary to this country. But, far from letting him preach his message, the government threw him into prison where he was mercilessly tortured for a long time, and was forced to eat pork. (At this point, Huḍūr[ra] pointed to the missionary in question, who was present in the audience and asked him to rise from his seat so that others could see him.) For almost two years this missionary was kept in captivity in various places—Tashkent, Ashgabat and Moscow—and while in prison, he was subjected to so much torture that he lost his mental balance. Then he was pushed across the border into Iran from where the British Embassy informed the Government of India about him and the information was sent to me, and at our request he was repatriated to India at our expense.

There are political reasons why the Communists disallow religious missionary work, which we need not pursue here. But the issue remains that a minority needs to make tremendous sacrifices to win over the majority to its religion. It certainly involves great personal sacrifice as well as expense of making available the religious literature, etc. But the Communist system leaves no margin for people to spend anything at all on such things.

Take the case of the Ahmadiyya Movement, for example. We are a very small community, but our aim is to win over the whole world for Islam. In order to convey Islam's message to 170 million Russians, massive expenditure on missionary activity and preparation of literature is required. But we would be unable to fulfil our mission if Communists take away all earnings beyond what is needed to meet the barest necessities of life. Communism, besides, opposes religious missionary activity because, from its point of view, this does not constitute useful activity. Only operating a machine, tilling the soil, or working in factories, etc.—which yield an economic return— are, regarded as productive work. It dismisses religion as consisting of superstitions and foolish fantasies, and, as such, does not recognise propagation of true faith as useful work. There is, therefore, no reason for the State to permit such parasitic activity.

Thus there is a direct clash between the Islamic conception of life and the communist viewpoint. To a Muslim, it matters little if he has to go hungry so long as he succeeds in improving his chances in the life to come. And, he wishes the same for his brethren—if they do not win God's pleasure, their life would have been in vain no matter how much wealth they acquired in this worldly life.

Anyone who holds this belief would be duty-bound to help his misguided brethren to provide something for the Hereafter. But Communism takes away all surplus wealth in the name of protecting the country, thus leaving everyone to suffer a spiritual death. As noted earlier, Islam shares with the Communist order the principle of ensuring that everyone gets adequate food, clothing and shelter and has access to education and medical relief. The government must, therefore, have sufficient public revenues to discharge these responsibilities. However, apart from taking away surplus funds, Communism forbids propagation of our faith. In short, we give them our support and we do so because this is the teaching of the religion we follow; but Communism instead of being thankful to this religion, repays the kindness by depriving it of all opportunities for growth on the pretext that it amounts to useless activity and a burden on the national economy.

Had Communism openly and honestly clashed with religion, we would have differed with it but could have had little basis for complaint. But the Communists profess to be unconcerned with religion while, by indirect and underhand means, they try to minimise its influence and stifle its spread. They seek to enter our hearts and homes as trusted friends, but betray this trust by covertly destroying the objects that we treasure most. The reality becomes apparent only when it is too late. If Communism declared openly that it did not recognise a life in the Hereafter, it attached no value to this idea, and it would not permit individuals to preach their religion, whoever accepted Communism would do so with eyes open. But outside Russia these vital aspects of the system are deliberately kept out of sight, behind a fraudulent claim that Communism is only an economic philosophy that has no concern with religion and does not clash with it. Missionary activity comprises a fundamental and most vital part of religion, which could not be sustained when the public is denied the right to raise funds for maintaining it and religion itself cannot long survive. In short, Communism aims to strangle the propagation of religion and seeks to establish an irreligious social order.

Now consider another aspect of this question. Suppose a Muslim said that he wanted nothing from the Soviet State but be allowed to dedicate his life to the service of religion and to visit every Russian town and village to convey Islam's message. Would the Soviet State permit him to do so? Would his activities not be stopped by straightaway throwing him in prison? There can be only one answer to this question. The Communist government of Russia would not hesitate to use force against such a person. He would be locked up in jail and told either to undertake some 'useful work' for his living or go without food or clothing. In other words, if I dedicated my life to God and the study of the Holy Quran and Hadith (a study indispensable for me if I desire to improve my life in the Hereafter), Communism would view this as sheer waste of time and an excuse to live at others' expense.

A Muslim must refuse to be tied down to the ultra materialistic theories of Communism in matters of such transcending spiritual importance. He must insist on his right to be guided by the Holy Quran, which deems it necessary that among the Muslims there should always exist a body of men entirely devoted to the task of calling people to the right path and dissuading them from the wrong. Allah the Almighty says:[24]

---

[24] *Sūrah Āl-e-'Imrān*, 3:105, (publishers)

وَلْتَكُن مِّنكُمْ أُمَّةٌ يَدْعُونَ إِلَى الْخَيْرِ وَيَأْمُرُونَ بِالْمَعْرُوفِ وَيَنْهَوْنَ عَنِ الْمُنكَرِ ۚ وَأُولَٰئِكَ هُمُ الْمُفْلِحُونَ ۞

That is: O Muslims there must always be among you a group of people who free themselves from the materialistic pursuits to oversee the religious obligations. The duties assigned to such people would be that they will enjoin piety, motivate people to carry out good deeds, and forbid them from immorality.

In other words, Islam requires that a group of Muslims must be totally dedicated for this task. It is true that Islam accords no special privileges to such devotees, but they are assigned certain specific duties that they must carry out. While there is no priesthood in Islam, it does call for a religious order to spread its message. Christianity gives to the priest some additional privileges. But in Islam even those who serve religion have the same rights as everyone else, though their work is well-defined and is of a religious nature—to spread Islam and to plant it deep in the hearts of people so that they live up to it and to regard this duty as their highest purpose in life. Deprived of the spiritual nucleus of such a body of men, the Islamic order could not survive, for it requires people who understand its rules and regulations and who are willing to spread its ideals.

Among the world's religions, Islam is the most detailed, encompassing a comprehensive and complete law. It has a clear teaching on the devotion and worship due to God, a clear teaching in regard to the economic aspect of man's life, his political activities, moral and ethical questions, social relationships dealing with employment, education, family life and business dealings, law of inheritance, international affairs, judiciary precepts and procedures and a host of regulations designed to cover every conceivable contingency in human life. Each of these aspects demands a thorough study, which is impossible unless a body of capable men make it the object of their lives. If such persons were stamped out of existence, from whom would the ordinary people learn? What would they learn? And how would Islam spread in the world?

Tafsīr [commentary of the Holy Quran] is a vast branch of learning in itself that cannot exist independently of competent scholars devoted to its study, involving a thorough grasp of the earlier works and traditions, a command over the language, its usage and grammar, familiarity with the hadith, [sayings of the Holy Prophet[sa]], and a study of comparative Religion, Arab and Jewish history, and the Bible. All this cannot be achieved without a lifelong effort, though, of course, a person might be blessed with this knowledge directly from the divine source. But this, is very rare—perhaps once in a century. Others can acquire it only through diligent study based upon righteousness. In the Communist State, such work is not considered work at all—it would not permit anyone to spend twelve years in studying and then a lifetime of teaching it to others. Such a person would be imprisoned or deprived of food and lodging, as he is a useless burden on the State.

The situation is similar with respect to the branch of learning known as hadith. It involves careful study of dozens of works and their expositions, Arabic usage and grammar, and careful scrutiny of the chain of narrators in the case of each hadith. Without a proper study of hadith—a life-long activity—adequate knowledge of the details of Islamic teaching is impossible. Similarly, in the case of the branches of learning known as *fiqah* [religious knowledge], *qaḍā* [jurisprudence], history, *taṣawwuf* [mysticism], and teachings of

Islam in social and economic activities. All these are branches of study that cannot be ignored without turning Islam into a dead letter, and no Muslim worth the name could ever be reconciled to such a state of affairs. But there is no place for such scholars or their students under Communism. The State would consider them unproductive and grant them no allowances. People themselves would have no means for supporting them through voluntary private donations—as is the experience in countries like India, China and Arabia. The truth is that between Islam and the other religions, on one side, and Communism, on the other, there is a fundamental difference in the conception of what constitutes work.

Our view is that a machine operator, a person propagating or teaching religion, and a recipient of religious education are all engaged in useful work. Communism, however, accords this status only to a machine operator, while those teaching or learning religion are regarded as parasites. To teach the alphabet is useful work according to the Communist view but to teach the profound truth— لا اله الا الله محمد رسول الله 'There is none worthy of worship but Allah and Muhammad is His Messenger'—is waste of time and energy.

Thus, while we are in accord with Communism that only useful workers may have their labour rewarded, we cannot accept at all that no work is to be considered useful unless the Communists so certify. In the estimation of Communists, to work for the betterment of one's spiritual life is no work at all; to teach or learn the Holy Quran, *hadith*, *fiqah*, *tafsīr*, *taṣawwuf*, and to teach morality is no work. In the eyes of a Muslim, on the other hand, these things are far more precious than life itself. To ensure proper study of religion and adequate effort is made for its propagation, thousands of scholars are needed in a country like Soviet Russia with its Muslim population of 30 million. But Communist Russia would only look upon them as shirkers, idlers and worthless people, who are a burden on society, and need to be quickly eliminated.

These two views stand poles apart; it is impossible to reconcile them. Undoubtedly, some do claim to serve religion, but they are impostors, who do not practice what they claim. But a person who really and truly serves religion at the cost of personal comfort and gain deserves to be recognised as a true leader; he holds a position similar to that of the soul in relation to the body; he is our greatest benefactor. To the Communist, however, such persons are only despicable scamps or idlers, and traitors to the nation, who should be imprisoned or driven out of the country.

There is someone who, in our estimation, stands so high that the mightiest rulers of this earth carry less weight and value in our eyes than the dust on his feet. It is the deepest and fondest desire of our hearts to sacrifice our lives for him. —He is Muhammad[sa], the greatest benefactor of mankind, who illuminated the human soul with Divine Light. But, according to the Communist way of thinking, he would be considered (God forbid) as a burden upon his people, as were all the chosen ones of God before him—Jesus[as], Moses[as], Abraham[as], Krishna[as], Ramchandra[as], Buddha[as], Zoroaster[as], Guru Nanak[rh] and Confucius[as]. The Soviet regime would, God forbid, send all such persons into workshops to make shoes or clothing for farm and factory workers or assign them the task of cutting other people's hair. Failing that, they would be deprived of food since according to them they are parasites and a burden on the national economy.

Communism does, however, recognise the work of painters and sculptors as 'creative artists', but considers work done to uplift people's souls or morals as utterly useless. As we all know, man does not live by bread alone, and food by itself cannot give him the peace of mind. The world is full of people who, if prevented from praying to God, would have no peace, no matter what luxuries of life were placed at their disposal.

It is indeed odd that Communism recognises it as work when labourers spend a few hours in factories, but then go out to dissipate themselves in drink, cinema or dance-halls. Photography and music, too, are considered useful pursuits, but moral improvement and purification of the soul constitute no work at all.

Some time ago, Marshal Malinovsky was asked about his sons interests. He responded laughing, 'They are interested in photography, music and keeping rabbits'. A child of fifteen, in other words, who spent his time in photography and music or in scampering after pet rabbits deserves to be fed and taken care of by Communism. But the Holy Prophet Muhammad[sa], Jesus Christ[as], Moses[as], Krishna[as], Buddha[as], Zoroaster[as] and Guru Nanak[rh] (God forbid) are considered as parasites and danger to society. They are not worthy of being called 'workers.'

History provides no example that matches the selfless, ceaseless labour of love undertaken by these great moral benefactors of mankind. But for their toil and effort, humanity would have lacked social cohesion, which depends on the sense of moral obligations that developed only after colossal sacrifices on the part of these great Teachers, who worked and suffered for the human cause day and night. Yet Communism condemns them as worthless people and places them far lower in the scale than drunkards and debauches who work in factories for hardly eight hours a day, then give themselves up to all sorts of low and vulgar pursuits.

In short, there is no place for these great and noble souls in the Communist system. I cannot speak for others, but I do know that in a state that provides no place for the Holy Prophet Muhammad[sa], there can be none for me. We can regard as ours only that country or regime that accords to the Holy Prophet Muhammad[sa] a place of ultimate honour. A country closed to him must be a country closed to every true Muslim. Communism might cover up this stark reality from religious believers to win their sympathy and allegiance, but it can never attract them if the truth is told. Communists are prone to assert that they do not oppose any religion. The Communists might declare that they do not oppose religion, but in reality that is not the case. Their oral pronouncements are therefore no more than lies.

Regarding this point, it may be mentioned that Russia obstructs religious education on grounds that parents have no right to impart religious knowledge to their children and thereby influence their leanings. Communists argue that it would be cruel to allow parents to influence their children, as they lack judgement to freely decide for themselves. Children must be allowed to choose for themselves about religion upon reaching adulthood. On the surface it seems to be a fair and reasonable demand, but in reality it is cruel and terrifying. All religions seek to propagate a positive message—the existence of God—whereas nonbelievers deny it. Those with a positive message have the responsibility to spread it; nonbelievers need do nothing. Thus, the Communist position is not one of equality, but is deceptive and unjust. It can be likened to a situation where a man is barred from telling his child about his being the father, but is then given assurance that no one else would be allowed to deny his fatherhood.

If a child is not taught the alphabet or history, he is bound to remain ignorant, similarly for religious education. As stated earlier, religion has a positive message to impart, but nonbelievers are just deniers. By not allowing religious education, the deniers are the ones who achieve their goal. Thus, while Communism claims to be impartial on religion, it is only committing treachery. This is not impartiality or equality in treatment, but fraud and deception. The Holy Quran plainly proclaims 'Teach man what he did not know.' As soon as you have ruled out the possibility of teaching, you put those so deprived at a disadvantage, and place them in a position of pre-Islamic days of ignorance, and prevent Muslims from carrying out their duty. There are some other points that arise in this connection, but as I am not addressing aspects of Communism that are not related to economics, I shall not go into them here.

Apart from the harm flowing from its opposition to religion, Communism is defective when judged on the basis of reason and common sense as well.

It is not in human power to establish complete equality for all, covering all aspects of life. Happiness does not depend on money alone, nor do contentment, solace and the peace of mind spring only from the satisfaction of material wants. Besides, given the same standards of living, the amount of pleasure derived must differ greatly from individual to individual. Given the same quality of meal, some people eat it with greater relish than others at the same table. The sense of taste, smell, eyesight, or general health varies among people. Intellectual and physical capabilities are a great source of self-confidence and consequent happiness, but no State action can make these factors equal for everyone. Our near and dear ones are a great source of happiness, but no regime can guarantee that wives, children, parents or friends of each individual would live equally as long. The presence of children around the hearth satisfies the deepest needs of human nature, but no one can guarantee that all married couples will have children, or have an equal number of children, or that the children will all live equally long, be equally healthy, or achieve equal success in life. The pangs of separation from a loved one can be a source of great pain. A mother who has lost her only child will not relish a sumptuous meal, whereas a poor mother who holds her child in her lap will enjoy even a simple meals more than a feast.

The intensity of emotions in regard to dear ones may be judged from the following incident in Lenin's life. The Russian Communist Party split into two groups at an early stage of its history because of some fundamental differences in viewpoints. The Mensheviks, who were led by Martove, held the view that on gaining political power, the Communist system must abolish capital punishment, but Lenin, who led the Bolsheviks—while accepting the principle—wanted to delay its adoption until after the Czar had been executed. The basic reason for Lenin's tougher stance was that the Czarist government had previously ordered his brother—to whom he was deeply attached—to be hanged in connection with a crime, and Lenin wanted to have his revenge on the Czar.

The suffering of our friends and relatives thus profoundly affects our happiness, and no one can take out an insurance against such suffering. It is therefore beyond the power of man to remove or level up inequalities in the countless aspects of human life, and the kind of equality that Communism rants about is little more than a delusion. Abiding happiness comes from the relationship with God alone, because all contingencies are under His control. You may grant food and clothing in equal amounts, but the man who lacks the relationship with God can have no peace. There are countless things whose presence or absence cause dissatisfaction, but it is entirely up to God to grant or withhold them.

2. *Communism Interferes with Property Rights*

Russia under the Czars was not an industrial country. It consisted of large country estates owned by hereditary nobles. Land therefore was the first concern of Communism in Russia, not industry. Whatever Karl Marx wrote about Capitalism concerned mainly big money and industry, as he was born and educated in Germany, which was far more industrialised. When Lenin and other Russian revolutionary leaders adopted his philosophy and tried to apply his theories to Russian conditions, they came up with the following principles:

1. All land belongs to the State;
2. Land must therefore be taken over by the State and be redistributed to those willing to till the soil;
3. Each land-holder should have just enough land that could be cultivated by him alone, and no more;
4. Land, as property of the State, must be utilized to its full potential. The cultivator, as agent of the State, must accept the decisions of the State regarding use of land.

RIGHT TO OWN LAND

Islamic teachings, the broad principles of which have already been explained, is that all land belongs to God who *recognises just titles to portions of it*, subject to the condition that, at the death of the titleholder, the land should be divided among stipulated heirs in specified proportions (one share for each boy, one-half share for the girl and one-third share for the parents) and that in no case must it be passed on to any single heir by excluding the others. In the absence of children, the land would be divided among brothers, sisters, and parents and, if there were no legitimate heir, the land would revert to God's representative, which is the State in this case. No one may bequeath more than one-third of his inheritance, with the condition that none of the stipulated heirs have any share in this one-third. This teaching is full of wisdom, because:

1. The right of ownership is recognised, therefore, every owner would be inclined to put their land to best use, as his livelihood depends on it.
2. Because the owner's children know that one day they too would be cultivating the land, they would strive to gain expertise in farming.
3. Even where there are large landholdings initially, they would be subdivided into smaller lots over time because of the law of inheritance.
4. Finally, because Islam maintains that all land belongs ultimately to God, no one may acquire it through illegitimate means.

Under non-Islamic systems, conquered territories are given away to the companions of conqueror or to those with influence. It is because of this system that the Norman conquerors were able to parcel out land in certain areas of England, Scotland and Ireland to chosen nobles, while leaving the inhabitants landless, with no place even to build their own homes. This situation persists in several areas to this day, where large owners rent out their buildings, but retain their power and influence. The same thing happened in France, Germany, Austria and Italy, though some improvement in the situation occurred following the Napoleonic wars. In the United States of America, too, as the country developed, a group of big land owners emerged through the simple expediency of dispossessing as many of the original inhabitants as they could manage and then continued to hold on to what they had gained, or rather usurped. And the same story repeated itself in Australia and Kenya, where English settlers took possession of hundreds of thousands of acres, leaving the natives landless.

As a result of the Islamic conquests in Arabia, the conquerors were given a portion of the land. Since in Arabia proper, arable land was limited, there was little danger of large illicit landowners to emerge. In Yemen and Syria however, both of which had a long established agricultural tradition, land was left in the possession of the original owners. Iraq, in contrast, was a sparsely populated, but fertile country that had been evacuated when the Persians moved back to their own country. Although some Generals in the victorious Islamic army did initially try to redistribute the land among the conquerors; Ḥaḍrat Umar[ra] disapproved of the idea. His reason was that he could foresee the harm it could do to succeeding generations. He, therefore, retained the vanquished land as government property. Similarly, in Egypt, original landowners were left in possession of the land.

In short, in the shape given to the Islamic Order at the outset, it was recognised that vacant lands that came under Muslim authority in conquered territories were to remain in the State's hands and be used in the general interest of all, instead of being distributed among the top leadership. This was done to avoid the emergence of a landed aristocracy, as happened in Europe. During later periods, it is true, the Islamic teaching was not fully observed, but Muslim rulers were never altogether freed from its influence. In India, too, when the Muslim rule came to the country, the land was left with the old owners whose tenure was preserved. Only vacant land was taken over by the State. All of the large estates found in India today were created later under the British rule. The new rulers were eager to settle matters and gain influence in the country, regardless of whether this was achieved through favour or fear. In most cases, the new governments in Bengal and Uttar Pradesh bestowed title to the *tehsildars* [tax collecting agents] over areas found in their jurisdiction. This was a terrible injustice to the real owners of those lands.

Thus, the Islamic system applies to land ownership in a manner similar to its application in other economic spheres, i.e., there is no place for large land owners and the government cannot create a class of large land owners by redistributing state land. It is another matter that a person might purchase additional land, but there is not much scope for this either. If it is a trader, he is unlikely to purchase land as he might make more money in trade. If he is already a landowner, his means to purchase additional land are in any case limited and not significant enough to harm the country's economic condition. Furthermore, thanks to the laws of inheritance, the size of land ownership would decline within one or two generations.

ISLAMIC APPROACH TO REDUCE LANDHOLDINGS AS COMPARED WITH COMMUNIST APPROACH

It should also be borne in mind that Islam does not allow anyone—not even someone who has no heirs and has made a will—to dispose of more than one-third of his property according to his own wishes. If he does have heirs, the land would be distributed in successive generations. If someone wishes to bequeath one-third to an heir for family prestige, Islam would not permit it—because none of the heirs are permitted to take any part of this one-third. Consequently, large land holdings under the Islamic system are virtually impossible. Even someone without an heir cannot bequeath more than one-third to anyone. The remainder will revert to the State, and thus be of benefit to the public at large.

Another strength of this system is that while it prevents a landed aristocracy from interfering with the uplift of the poor, it does not curtail individual freedom. In fact, it leaves everyone free to develop intellectually, promote his family life, and allows him to do whatever is necessary for the preparation for the life to come. In contrast, the measures adopted by Communism, to translate its ideology into practice, destroy individual liberty, kill domestic harmony, and deny any chance of serving one's religion. What is more, Communism has utterly failed to implement what it originally sought.

In regard to land, Communism held that all land belonged to the State, an approach that made the State the sole landowner, while transforming the farmers into mere wage earners. Communism thereby placed landowners at a disadvantage compared to merchants and industrialists who, to a certain extent, were given property rights over what they possessed. Because the State was the sole owner of land, Communism held that the State was entitled to direct the farmer what to sow and where to sow it. Moreover, as some farmers had more experience in handling certain crops, the State was entitled to send them wherever their expertise was needed.

When these ideas were implemented country-wide, farmers came to realise that:

1. Their status had been reduced to that of mere labourers, lower than that of merchants or artisans;
2. Their family life had been deprived of all stability and the right of their descendents to enjoy the fruits of their labour had been usurped;
3. They were liable to be moved from their farms and sent off to unknown places at any time;
4. They were no longer able to choose their crops in order to stay self-sufficient. Instead, they were made to cultivate in accordance with the State's dictates. This destroyed the previous system under which villages and towns were self-sufficient.

Because of these developments, the landowners rebelled and maintained their resistance for a number of years, resulting in a fall in agricultural output. Finally, Stalin abrogated that system and re-established the old system that provided for the right of private ownership over land, along with some latitude in cultivating what the landowners desired. Although the rebellion subsided, this decision on the part of the Bolshevik leader demonstrated once and for all that the Communist system was seriously flawed. Consequently, Stalin's enemies accused him of betraying the Communist principles as laid down by Lenin. Stalin's response to this accusation was that the key goal of Communism was the establishment of a proletarian regime. No harm was done if lesser principles were sacrificed in the attainment of the ultimate goal. In any case, this instance showed that as a permanent system of political economy, Communism failed to translate its policies regarding landownership into action, and that in tackling this question the Communists had to borrow ideas from other systems.

This glaring failure of the Communist system demonstrates the inherent superiority of the Islamic economic system, and shows that Communism is not a principled philosophy, rather just a political movement seeking to strengthen Russia. To assert itself as an alternative to religion is a violation of truth and rectitude.

Stephen King-Hall, a member of the British Parliament, recently visited Russia and published an article in the 'Soviet Union News', in which he stated that Russia currently had two goals: First, the reconstruction of Russia, and second, to make it the best and richest country in the world. Communism is therefore basically a political movement with the primary objective of making Russia powerful.

3. Communism Stifles Growth of Knowledge

Although all are assured of food and clothing in the Soviet regime, its adopted measures also give rise to another grave fault in the system, i.e. intellectual progress will gradually die out. Because workers' wages and salaries in this system are barely adequate to pay for food, shelter and clothing, leaving very little for foreign travel. This is a critical component of education that contributes to the development of scientific and technical knowledge and to the progress of civilisation. The Holy Quran has laid great emphasis upon *sair-fil-arḍ*, that is, travelling in various parts of the earth. When the Russian people had economic freedom, they saved a part of their income for travel to different countries. What they learned from foreign travels helped to enrich their country and contributed to national progress.

This is the path nature has established for promoting progress and many nations have benefitted by adopting it. The Holy Quran has also enjoined travel to different lands; for without it, one's perspective remains constricted. But because of the Communist system, it is now impossible for Russians to freely travel abroad, and the same thing will happen wherever Communism spreads. Its inevitable consequence would be an intellectual decline. Since the Revolution, one does occasionally come across a Communist government representative, but it is extremely rare to meet an ordinary citizen from a communist country.

As the Imam of a large and far-flung religious Community, I have a wide network of contacts. I have not had the opportunity of meeting an independent Russian communist, though one does occasionally encounter representatives of the Soviet government. This is the consequence of the Soviet policy of not leaving any money in the hands of ordinary citizens beyond what they require to meet the expense of food, clothing and shelter.

It is sometimes said that the country can have access to foreign ideas and inventions through visits of government officials, but this is in fact not so. For one thing, a government official is confined to pursuing only matters related to the purpose of his travel. Secondly, a person travelling on his own volition, interest and freely interacting with other people is quite different from someone travelling on official duty. Finally, people-to-people interaction can be a source of intellectual growth and instrumental in promoting peace and understanding. The Soviet system precludes that possibility altogether.

Ordinary Russians that one comes across outside of Russia are usually emigrants who left their country during the Revolution, or are Russian agents engaged in propaganda for the Soviet State. The latter might claim to be independent citizens, unconnected to the government, but it is only a ruse to make their propaganda more effective. It only takes a little common sense to see that ordinary Russians cannot afford luxuries, such as foreign travel, because the State does not leave any spare money in their possession

Some time back, during my travel from Karachi to Lahore, a friend informed me that a Russian—who was travelling in the air-conditioned compartment on the same train—was claiming to be a private tourist, but was speaking strongly in favour of Communism. I asked my friend to tell this gentleman that his claim was utterly false. In the Russian's eyes, I would be considered as a big landowner but I could afford to travel only in second class. As there were no landowners left in Russia, the traveller must either be a farmer or an ordinary labourer, which would suggest that he was most certainly not a rich man himself. In that case, how would he explain his travel in such luxury? If a Russian worker or a farmer could travel in an air-conditioned railway coach, how could he protest against landowners who could barely afford to travel in second class? All the pious wrath of Russian Communists against Indian landowners or capitalists was therefore just hypocrisy.

4. Force Needed to Uphold Communism

The fourth flaw of Communism is that whenever the system encounters a serious difficulty or challenge, it gets replaced by dictatorship, with consequences far worse than before. The reason is that by destroying independent thinking, the system is bereft of new ideas that might help to overcome the challenge. As such, when the process of decline sets in or the system collapses altogether, there would be nothing, other than dictatorship, to fill the vacuum so created. Germany accepted Hitler, mainly because of the Communist movements that had swept the country. The experience of the French Revolution also supports that viewpoint. As the first wave of popular fervour over the newfound freedom receded, it gave rise to an autocrat like Napoleon. No one from among the ordinary people could assume the control of affairs under a democratic system.

Communism may choose to call itself a proletarian or a totalitarian regime. There is little doubt that this kind of system eventually and inevitably leads to dictatorship. In fact, the current situation is that although they claim to support representative government, in reality they do not share governance with ordinary citizens. There has only been dictatorship since the inception of Communism in Russia. Lenin was the first dictator, who was succeeded by Stalin; Molotov may well be the third dictator, and so on. In any case, such regimes cannot survive without the use of force, and the Russian experiment stands testimony to that.

5. *Interest, a Part of Communist Philosophy*

The fifth flaw of Communism is that it has not rejected the institution of interest as part of its philosophy. It is claimed that there are no private banks in Soviet Russia that operate on the basis of interest. I do not at the moment have any certain knowledge that this is actually the case. But the absence of banks that run on the basis of interest is an entirely different matter from rejecting interest as something fundamentally wrong. The absence of such banks may be due to a number of reasons: lack of facilities, general ignorance on the part of the public in regard to the working of banks, or just expediency. When the necessary facilities are installed, the public gets educated about the banking system, or when the opportunistic policy is abandoned, individual banks may start operating throughout the country. But when something is forbidden as a matter of principle, no change in circumstances can make it lawful or acceptable. Communism does not put interest under this absolute ban.

There is no prohibition of interest in the communist literature, which leads me to conclude that Communism is not fundamentally opposed to the institution of interest. I find, besides, that the Soviet government borrows from other governments that lend only on interest. Thus, it is clear Communism is not against interest—indeed, it accepts its use. During this war, the Russian government borrowed from Russian people, which I surmise must have been on interest.

If I am correct that Communism is not fundamentally opposed to interest (in fact, various developments leave no other conclusion possible), it must be conceded that the dearth of interest-based transactions in the country is only a temporary phenomenon and a consequence of the extraordinary changes that occurred since the overthrow of the old order. With the expansion of Russian trade and industrial development, the Soviet State too would increasingly resort to interest-bearing loans, just as in other European countries. Accordingly, for the successful prosecution of wars and industrial development, the branches of the state bank will be established in the country, and the institution of interest would take the country from Communism to Capitalism, just as it did in the other Western countries.

6. Adoption of Prevailing Exchange Rate System

The sixth flaw of the Communist economic system—one that will not let it supersede capitalism—lies in its adoption of the exchange rate mechanism, which emerged out of banks' manipulation and government interference. Communism not only supports this mechanism, but has chosen to act according to its dictates. As it is, the exchange rate (which is the relative price of two currencies) is no longer determined by a country's balance of trade, but is fixed by the great economic powers. In fixing the exchange rate, these powers pursue basically their own self-interest and trade strategy. They take into account not only the current balance of trade but also the development of future commercial relations. As far as the weaker or poorer economies are concerned, their exchange rates are in the hands of banks.

Weaker countries often complain about the prevailing system but their protests go unheeded, and they continue to face a disadvantage in trade, as they lack sufficient economic influence. As things stand, an exchange rate between two currencies is essentially artificial and can be utilised to their advantage by banks as well as governments. As a result, international trade, instead of being governed by supply and demand conditions in the markets of commodities and precious metals, is driven by the exchange rates between different currencies. Consequently, the trade of the weaker economies is subject to manoeuvring on the part of banks, while the trade of the stronger economies is influenced by political considerations. There is no doubt that the exchange rate system has facilitated commerce, and the growing volume of international trade would not be possible without a satisfactory system of exchange. But it is not necessary that for the exchange rates to be subject to politics and used as a means to exploit poor economies.

With careful consideration, it should be possible to adapt the old barter system—which was based on the exchange of goods, not the exchange rate—to meet the present-day requirements of trade, while protecting it from government interference. After due consultation with traders and government representatives, the exchange rate regime could be adjusted as needed, but its guiding principle must remain the exchange of goods rather than paper money.

After the war [of 1914–18], Germany manipulated its exchange rate and depreciated its currency so much that capital began to flow into the country from all over the world. And when it had built up large enough foreign exchange reserves to meet its commercial requirements, Germany just abolished its currency at little or no cost. This kind of measure could not have been possible under the barter system. Russia did attempt to follow in Germany's footsteps, but because of its lack of financial expertise and backward industry, it could not derive much benefit from it. An artificial exchange rate, in short, is a weapon that the strong can use to gain control over the trade of weaker countries and to make trade flow not in its natural directions but into channels of their choice.

By accepting the prevailing exchange rate system, Communist Russia in effect has left the foundation of capitalism intact. As a consequence, with the growth of its industries, the country would resort increasingly to this weapon to secure new markets, thereby gaining control over the trade of weaker countries. The Soviet State may of course amass great wealth this way, but in the process she would undermine the weaker economies and thus nullify the very principle that gave it birth:[25]

---

[25] Note: The author's above remarks were both profound and prescient. Soon after the time of this lecture, The International Monetary Fund (IMF) and the World Bank were established, and currency manipulation by any country was made unacceptable and subject to sanctions. (publishers)

7. Compulsion in Economic Matters

The seventh flaw is that the Communist system requires the use of force to run the economy, which ends up only hurting the country. It seeks to confiscate the wealth of the rich, leaving them with only the bare necessities of life. Irrespective of the merits or demerits of the objective, the issue is that Communism regards it legitimate to use force to pursue its objectives. Instead of relying on education and persuasion to make people gradually change their attitudes and become more compassionate towards the poor and accept the principle of equity, Communism, on coming to power, employed only force to deprive the rich of their wealth. Clearly, this process could not but rouse hatred for the system on the part of the dispossessed. Those who suffered in the process could hardly have any sympathy, instead of resentment, for the Communist system.

Without question, Islam too took away wealth from the rich, but it did not use force. It relied in the first place on persuasion, but it also went on to remove the incentives to amass wealth. This was followed by discouragement of excessive consumption as well as admonition to give zakat and charity to help the poor. Finally, wealth that still remained at the time of a person's death was distributed among heirs. Thus while both Communism and Islam sought equity, the former relied on forcefully taking away wealth from the rich, while Islam relied on persuasion. The result is that there is a significant cross-section of rich Russians living in other countries that oppose Communism for usurping their wealth and reducing some of them to a life of penury.

Communists are mistaken in thinking that there is no opposition to the communist system in other countries. They do not realise that the opposition is hushed only because the Western powers—America and England—need Russia's help in the war effort and are not prepared to allow criticism of Russia. As the war comes to an end, the Western governments will not be able to control the freedom of expression, and schemes for the elimination of the communist system will once again begin to emerge. (It may be noted that soon after this speech, the Second World War ended and criticisms of Communism became very strong, especially in the United States.)

8. *Communism Destroys Family Relations*

The eighth flaw in Communism is that it destroys home life and family relations, which will ultimately cause its decline. Communism virtually ignores the deep natural bonds between parents and their children, between brothers and sisters, and other close relations united by ties of blood. In its eagerness to indoctrinate them into Communism and to move them away from religion, it decided to treat children as belonging to the State. Instead of being raised in the care of the mother and father, the child is put completely under the government's control—at least according to the law. The result is that the family relations are totally disrupted. This state of affairs too cannot continue for long. It must change, for otherwise a Russian would cease to be a normal human being.

Although Communism appears at the moment to be firmly established in Russia, the fact is that the Communism's evident success is basically due to a reaction against the miseries wrought by the czarist regime. If Communism continues to be successful after the memory of those sufferings fades away, one could say that it succeeded in eliminating the natural bonds of love between parents and children and among the siblings.

Let the world beware that such bonds of love cannot be crushed. A day will dawn when a mother will be loved as a mother, a father will be honoured as a father, and a sister will get her due place. The hitherto suppressed bonds would surely reassert themselves. But right now, the system regards a man simply as a machine, not as a man. It has no respect for the feelings of a mother, a father, a sister, or any other relative. This concept of man as a piece of machinery could not survive for long. A time would come when this system would be overthrown and replaced by one that accords due recognition to filial bonds.

9. Communism Undervalues Intellectual Excellence

The ninth flaw of Communism is that it does not adequately recognise intellectual and mental capabilities, which causes Russians with those capabilities to emigrate to other countries in search of higher rewards. Bolshevism regards only manual labour as real work and dismisses intellectual endeavour as waste of time. Manual labour is undoubtedly important, but it is equally true that intellectual effort has importance of its own. Because it is an inherent human trait that people expect to be adequately rewarded for their services, Russia must modify its philosophy if it desires to avail itself of the services of its intellectual giants and scientists. Otherwise, they will slip out to other countries and seek recognition and reward denied to them in their own country. The discoveries and inventions of Russian scientists and engineers will be registered, patented and exploited not in Russia, but in America.

At present the Soviet government prevents its people from emigration through rigid control, but as Russia's contact with the outside world expands, these controls would have to be relaxed in the interest of foreign trade, if for nothing else. Those who might wish to escape would then have ample opportunity to do so. When Germany began to mistreat Jews, many escaped to America, which benefited from their knowledge and skills. Some of the chemicals, previously manufactured only in Germany, are now being produced in the USA. If Russia were to open its doors to outside contacts, dissatisfied scientists will have a chance to slip out. But if Russia remains closed, its culture will, for want of fresh intellectual stimulus, begin to wither and end up as a pool of stagnant water.

10. Rigid Control over Economy

The tenth flaw of system lies in the rigid control of the Russian economy. The provision of food and clothing is at present government responsibility, and so are industry and foreign trade. Because, Russia was industrially backward, it is not possible to assess the country's real economic progress. Nevertheless, one thing is quite clear even now. As long as the products of Russian industry remain shielded from foreign competition and barely meet domestic requirements, it would not be known whether the factories make profits or run at a loss.

What would happen to those industries when the home market gets saturated? Would production be reduced thereafter? Or would the expansion continue? If a limit on production were imposed, industry would sooner or later start to feel the crippling effect; continued expansion, on the other hand, would require foreign markets that could absorb the surplus at prices still profitable for Russian manufacturers. When that stage is reached, Russian industry would have to withstand the full force of foreign competition, and its success or failure would depend on how it performs. In any case, Russia from that point onward would end up behaving like any other imperialist country, bent on securing and controlling foreign markets—thereby belying its claim of freedom of choice.

To reiterate, there is at present little incentive to produce at the lowest cost because of the absence of international competition—and this could continue for some time. This situation is similar to the one where a woman grinds five kilos of grain manually, which makes her household happy at the amount of work she puts in. But it is only when she goes out to work that she comes to realise the true worth of her work, because she earns considerably more money. Similarly, so long as the Russians consume all that is produced within the country, they would not know whether the economy was progressing or declining. The country appears to be making economic progress right now, but the reality would dawn only when its industry reaches the limits of its expansion.

If it manages to survive that dire situation, there would follow another consequence that I describe below.

11. Focus on National Interests Instead of Universal Welfare

The fact that the communist system is concerned only with national interests—not universal interests—is another major weakness of the system. If Russia somehow succeeds in industrial development, it would be forced to implement a capitalist system that is stronger and even more dangerous for the world than the one it replaces. In the face of this great danger, I am at a loss to understand why a segment of our intelligentsia is so strongly in support of Communism. The fact is that Russia has presented collectivist ownership in a manner that others are easily impressed, but a time will come that its damage to the world will become obvious.

People are impressed that Communism has ensured provision of food and clothing for everyone—and that is something we too welcome—but the great danger that lurks in its shadow must not be disregarded. That danger is the prospect of the rise of a new capitalist system.

Russia boasts that between 1928 and 1937, it raised its industrial production by 625%... This is indeed a commendable achievement. Russian Communism also claims that, during the same period, the worth of Russian productive capital rose from ten billion roubles to 75 billion roubles, i.e. seven and a half times (the monetary value of rouble is very low at prenet). It also claims that in 1937, one-third of its national income was invested to expand its factories. This, too, is quite impressive. But the question is how long can Russia maintain this pace of expansion in an economy closed to foreign trade?

The present situation is that the Russian economy is quite self-sufficient, with only a low level of imports and exports. Its imports are meant basically to satisfy the requirements of its industry. This situation resembles that of an Indian farmer, who raises a little sugarcane, some lentils, a little rice, wheat and some oil seeds on his piece of land, and manages to subsist on these things. But obviously this situation cannot continue as economic and cultural progress takes place. At some point exposure to the outside world must be faced. If it had been possible to maintain economic self-sufficiency forever, the conflicts seen all over the world—which led to World Wars—would have never occurred. But the fact is that this state of self-sufficiency cannot continue indefinitely.

Prospect of Russia Emerging as Global Economic Shock

It is now universally acknowledged that no country can survive on its own. Experience underscores the imperative for a country to establish relations with other nations. Thus, if the Soviet Union cannot maintain economic progress under autarchy, it would be impelled to search for foreign markets to dispose of its industrial surplus. This became abundantly evident during the war when the Soviet Union had to rely heavily on imports of essential goods from America and Great Britain. If it maintains its pace of industrialisation, the Soviet Union would have to find new markets for its products. When that day arrives, would the Russian policy not assume the same characteristics and adopt the same methods as we have seen in the history of other imperial powers? To put it plainly, Russia would be compelled to make other countries, by some means or other, to buy Russian products in order to keep its labour employed and sustain its economic and industrial growth.

Experience of Other Imperialist Powers

We have seen that when it concerns granting India independence, rousing speeches are made in the Houses of Parliament, but when it concerns economic progress, the experts start pronouncing on the need for protecting the British interests.

No doubt, Russia's case would be quite similar, though with one important difference. In the case of Great Britain and America it is the private firms that compete, but in the case of Russia it will be the entire socialist system that would compete with the individual foreign trader. It will not willingly close its factories and allow unemployment to rise in the face of foreign competition, but it will adopt all means to make other countries buy its products. And it will direct the entire might of its state—which owns factories and wields total political power—towards achieving that end.

The economically weak neighbouring countries would be particularly vulnerable to the Soviet pressure. At that point, Russia would use all tactics that the big investors employ under capitalism. Since industry in Russia is under State control, the clout of the political power will also be wielded. At that stage, Russia would not just be concerned with protecting its commercial interests, it would also seek to raise the standard of its industry, protect its labour and factories, and attract foreign capital. Thus, the neighbouring economies would end up opening their economies to Soviet goods, as they did for the Western capitalists. But this time it would be a bigger economic shock for the world.

Sometimes an argument is made that the vulnerable countries could escape the onslaught of Russian competition by becoming allies of the Soviet Union and gain all the advantages of the communist system. But a little reflection would establish that this idea is not sound. In the first place, we should not forget that not many countries would put aside all other considerations aside and rush to join the Soviet Union simply to capture some economic gains. The Communists in various countries would, of course, be glad to see the Soviet system introduced everywhere, but it seems doubtful that many would submit their economies to Russian dictates. This would apply to Communists in Great Britain and America and to those of practically every other country. They have a preference, no doubt, for the Soviet system, but they are not eager at all to let Moscow run their country's affairs.

I cannot say anything about the thinking of Indian communists. We know from experience that they are not given to thinking through important issues and, generally, are not well educated. They are fond of sloganeering, but few understand the implications of their slogans. Many put thought and reflection aside and get carried away by their emotions. It is possible that a large majority of the Indian Communists would not object to India being absorbed into the Soviet Union, but Communists in the rest of the world are not so inclined, and believe that such a situation would bring about ruin and destruction for their countries.

Absence of Equality in Russian Occupied Territories

We should also observe that the quality of life enjoyed by European Russians differs significantly from that of people living in the Soviet territories outside Europe. I would meet all expenses if the Communist Party were to let one member of my Community visit Soviet Union and show to him that the poor in Bukhara have everything that the poor in Moscow have, in terms of housing, clothing, food, education and medical care. I am sure an inspection of life in the two towns would show that there is an appalling difference in the degree of well-being enjoyed by their inhabitants. The same observation applies to the other Russian territories in Asia. Only recently, an official announcement was made regarding schemes to ameliorate conditions in these territories, and that a special programme would be devised for future progress there. This statement should help to dispel the delusion that Soviet Russia treats its Asian citizens as well as its European citizens. Had this been so, the European and Asian territories of the Soviet Union would have reached a similar economic status.

Some people believe that because Communism is based on the principle of equality, the system would not betray itself by usurping the rights of the weak. This idea is no more than a delusion. The

Russian reticence till now in economic competition and in scramble for foreign territories has not been due to any ethical sense of right or wrong, but simply from its inability to assert its power. These policies will undergo a radical transformation as soon as it becomes strong enough to impose its will.

In fact, the change can already be observed. So long as Russia was preoccupied with domestic politics, Finland, Latvia, Lithuania and Estonia were free and independent. Russia boasted that it did not get involved in the internal affairs of other countries and that in pursuit of liberation, it had granted independence to all countries that so desired—namely Latvia, Lithuania and Estonia, Finland, Poland, and Georgia. It had also handed over Turkey a portion of Armenia that was originally a part of Turkey. But as soon as domestic unrest abated, Georgia was incorporated into the Soviet Union. On gaining further strength, it started to dispute Finland's border. This process continued until the Soviet Union came to occupy Latvia, Lithuania and Estonia. Portions of Rumania too were nibbled off, and Finland was overpowered and some parts of it were incorporated into the Soviet Union, leaving the rest of the country independent. Poland is being quietly appropriated now.

Russia has proclaimed publicly that a government that does not support its policies would not be tolerated at its borders. Only governments that are prepared to remain loyal and subservient to Moscow can remain in power in these countries. Under the cloak of security, there has been Russian interference in the affairs of Poland, Czechoslovakia and Rumania. Schemes have been set afoot to grab the oil fields in Persia. Turkey is being called upon to hand back portions of Armenia ceded to it earlier and Moscow has openly sought control of the Dardanelles.

Did the old imperial governments do anything different in their days of glory? Did they not, in fact, proceed more gently and tactfully? Were they not less blunt and less brutal? To be sure, Great Britain too has had an interest in the Dardanelles for a long time, but it never applied the degree of pressure on Turkey as Russia has done in just a few years. With this evidence, it is not wise to believe that Russia would not force its neighbouring countries into economic subjugation in the same way as the European traders did with the help of their governments. Events have proved that as soon as Russia gained power, its claims of political equality and freedom went by the board.

There is now no basis for accepting Russia's claim that it has no interest in other countries. Upon entering the world of politics, Communism changed its ideology and disregarded its own principles in favour of advancing its own interests. Georgia, Bokhara, Finland, Latvia, Lithuania, and Estonia have all been occupied and brought under its political authority. Schemes are being prepared to gain influence in Iran and Turkey, and for the break up of China.

Can the occupation and subjugation of these countries be called equality and freedom of conscience? Why would Finland permit that a part of its territory be absorbed into Russia? Why was the freedom of Latvia, Lithuania and Estonia trampled underfoot? Why was it necessary that these countries should sacrifice their own independence to safeguard White Russia? Was it incumbent upon Georgia and Bokhara to get incorporated into the Russian empire? If this was for the cause of liberty and freedom, why did the opposite not take place? Why was not a part of Russia handed over to Finland, and other parts given to Poland, Rumania, Turkey and Iran to strengthen their defences? Surely, from the viewpoint of security, these smaller countries merited additional territory more than Russia did.

The fact is that Russia remained un-aggressive only as long as it lacked the power. Once it gained the power, Russia did not hesitate to devour the smaller states on grounds that it needed to strengthen its borders. If this were a valid reason, it could also be used by America to justify retaining control over the Japanese Islands. The reality is that those with power can always present excuses to justify their actions. As they say, 'might is right.'

Given this record of Russian approach in international politics, how can we hope that Russia would take a more egalitarian and just approach in the economic sphere? For those who think that political decisions are different [from economic decisions] the question can be posed differently: if Russia really loves equity why does it seek to occupy Iran's oil fields. Is this fair to Iran, considering that the country itself needs oil to support its poor and hungry people? If the interests and welfare of the weak have any value in Russia's eyes, as the Communists claim, then, Russia should have, for example, lent money to Iran free of interest so that Iran could develop its oil resources. It should be obvious, then, that the objective of Russia is to deprive Iran of the benefit of its oil fields to promote its own interests.

Some people argue that the British too have taken possession of Iran's oil fields. This is not a good argument, because the wrong done by one does not justify the same for someone else. If Britain is to be condemned for its actions, one should also condemn Russia. Russian actions demonstrate that its policies are in reality no different from the policies followed by other imperial powers. If Russia subscribes to the principle of equality, it should hand over oilfields of Baku to Iran on the ground that Iran must have the same rights as Russia. But Russia has no interest in such 'equality'.

Russia is still at an early stage of industrialisation. When it has advanced, we can expect to see that it would promote its industrial interests in other countries in a manner that has not been witnessed before. The reason is that Communism has only crushed individual capitalism, but it has nurtured and promoted collective capitalism, which is a very dangerous development. America passed the anti-trust laws precisely to curb this kind of development.

State Capitalism More Dangerous Than Earlier Imperialists

Experience shows that individual businesses are never as successful as companies, and companies are never as successful as trusts and trusts never as powerful as cartels. But companies that are backed or owned by state—as is the case in Russia—could assume power that no individual companies or even weak economies can achieve. Smaller economies, and even bigger economies, can manage to deal with individual private companies, but the state-run collective capitalism is altogether a different matter.

Large industrial countries always sought economic influence in small and weak economies, but it still remained possible for such countries to have their own capitalists. Because competition was between individuals, some businesses in smaller countries could withstand the competition from the bigger and better organised enterprises. Great Britain is one of the most highly industrialized countries, but that did not deter firms in Holland, Belgium and

Switzerland to compete with British firms, simply because the competition was between firms rather than countries. To put it differently, the British army can be expected to prevail over (say) Belgium in a confrontation, but every individual British soldier may not be able to overcome every Belgian soldier.

Private capitalism does have its dangers, but it does leave the weak some breathing space. However, when pitted against State Capitalism, the weaker and smaller economies have little chance of survival. This is analogous to an army equipped only with clubs having to take on an army equipped with machine guns. But State Capitalism —under which the entire economic and political might of one country is pitted against individual traders and manufacturers of another country—threatens to destroy the world economic order.

In short, Russian Communism has raised the prospect of a very dangerous form of Capitalism, and there are only two ways to deal with that threat:

1. One possibility is that the entire world adopts the same economic system and becomes a part of the Soviet Union, thereby ending the competition between unequal. Is there any possibility that such a development will take place? Would Great Britain, America and France be prepared to join the Soviet Union so that they could escape the onslaught of Russian competition? Even if that were conceivable, would this ensure that they would gain rights and privileges similar to those enjoyed by Russians themselves? Since that is unlikely, this really is no solution.

2. The other solution could be for each country to adopt the communist system, but retains its independence. If this were to happen, it would mean that state-owned enterprises would be pitted against each other—a situation that would be even more dangerous. While industrial enterprises of one country competed with individual enterprises of another country earlier, the state enterprise of one country would now compete with the state enterprise of another. Were this eventuality to materialise, we would face continuous warfare instead of occasional wars relieved by varying periods of peace. Commercial caravans would move across the globe, but would require armed forces to defend them. Trade and commerce would be conducted between government officials and not company managers. In such a world, smaller and weaker countries would lose their independence and end up turning into hunting grounds for the bigger, more powerful countries. The major industrial powers would continue to compete, but the competition would be between the governments, not their individual firms.

It is no more than a delusion to suppose that when such a stage is reached people everywhere would rise to the occasion and conclude a just and lasting peace. Russia today is not prepared to share its wealth with the less fortunate. There is no reason to expect that things will be different when it becomes wealthier. If it were disposed that way, it would not have set its eyes on controlling Iran's oilfields.

Russian Claims of Equality Among Nations Belied by its Actions

By joining the Big Three, Russia has clearly deviated from its stated principle of equality among nations. Where do the smaller and weaker nations stand against the Big Three—no more than a weakling confronting a wrestler. If Communist Russia were true to principle of absolute equality, it should have sided with the weak nations and insisted that it would not accept any difference in treatment among nations. If men are equal as individuals—that is equal in their rights as human beings—then it follows that all countries, no matter whether they are big or small, are equal in their rights and are entitled to their own healthy and happy life, safe from interference and humiliation.

Russia should have asserted the principle in inter-governmental bodies that all governments—weak and powerful—must have equal voice in protecting their rights. But Russia did not do so, and agreed to settle all important issues through consultations among the Big Three. By its action, Russia demonstrated that its voice must carry greater weight than the voice of smaller countries such as Belgium and Holland. If nations could not have equal rights, how could individuals expect equal treatment? Surely, moral and ethical standards must not differ in their application to individuals and nations. Thus, Russia's claim of equality has no substance and is mere show.

If a big government deserves preferential treatment, why should an expert technician or trader not have an advantage over an inexperienced technician or trader? Giving preferential treatment to a larger country could in fact be more harmful than allowing an individual to excel because of his special skills. Any in-equality which is created can be redressed with Islam's fine principles as discussed above.

This brings to mind an incident concerning one of India's leaders when several Indian political leaders gathered to deliberate on some a matters. The late Sir Sikander Hayat Khan and Sir Feroze Khan Noon invited me to take part in the meeting, which was held at Simla and was attended by about seventy or eighty leaders from all over the country. One of the leaders was rather annoyed with the size of the assembly, and said in his speech that such important matters could not conveniently be discussed or settled in large gatherings. He then proposed that only the 'leaders of leaders' should meet and let others know of the decision.

This is exactly Russia's position—that the decisions reached by the Three Big should be accepted by all others who lack the right to participate in these meetings. The sole reason for this is that Russia is a military power, while countries like Belgium, France and Holland are less powerful. If the military might is the only reason for giving weight to Russia's voice, it seems highly unlikely that Russia would be prepared to accept others in its economic programme. A country that accords little value to other countries' views concerning peace cannot be expected to provide food and clothing to them. Once its industry advances, Russia can be expected to seek 'mandates' over its markets instead of equal participation.

In short, the Soviet Union does not really stand for 'death to capitalism'—that is only an illusion in the minds of some people. Its real slogan is: Death to capitalism where individuals own property and long live the state capitalism of Russia. The consequence of this state of affairs can be predicted—it was possible to withstand the power and influence of individual capitalists, but nobody would be able to compete with the state-run capitalism.

BARRIERS TO FOREIGN INFLUENCES IN RUSSIA

It seems that Russia is aware of its basic weakness and tries to shield itself by restricting contacts with foreign countries. In an article published in the June issue of *The Soviet Union*, Mr. Stephen King-Hall, a member of the British Parliament, reported his impressions based on his recent visit to Russia. He wrote that the Russian Government did not wish that the Russian people should be exposed to Western ideas or thinking. He went on to say that it was only through official channels—not directly—that one could get an idea of the Russian way of life, and that this state of affairs would continue for some time.

Russian isolation was evident during the recent visit of a group of Russian expert who came along with some Americans to this country. The Russians were surprised to find that in India one could travel freely, while in their own country, people had little money to travel on their own. They felt as though they had been transported to a different world. This instance reflected Russia's lack of exposure to other countries. Obviously, the Russians cannot be kept in 'cold storage' indefinitely; one day the wall of isolation would crumble and the world would witness a profound transformation.

Russian Claims of Practising Equality Among its Citizens are Not Credible

I have my doubts about equality in Russia, but since the information about the actual situation is very scanty, one cannot be sure. I do know that ordinary Russian soldiers wear worn-out uniforms. I have learned this from our Ahmadi officers and soldiers who were posted in places where they had contact with the Russian army. According to them, the uniforms worn by the soldiers from the Asian part of the Soviet Union were particularly shabby. By contrast, the uniforms worn by Russian Marshals—as can be seen from their pictures in the newspaper—are elegant, resplendent with very expensive medals. The cost of these medals alone dispels any the notion of equality in the Soviet Union.

The state of equality in Russia can be gauged from a banquet Mr. Stalin gave in honour of Mr. Churchill when he visited Moscow during the war. Mr. Churchill, upon his return to England, said that he wished his capitalist country could afford to feed him on the same sumptuous scale as he had seen in a country with a proletarian Government. If equality really exists in Moscow, does an ordinary Russian get the same lavish dinners as are offered at state banquets? If not, it is evident that Russia has not resolved the problem of inequality, nor is there a prospect that it will in future.

The lavishness displayed at state banquets cannot be rationalised on grounds of necessity. During the war, state banquets in England were quite simple. Russia could have kept the banquet simple, but their real motivation was to impress Mr. Churchill with Russia's grandeur. It is this attitude that frustrates the spirit of equality. This incident also suggests that the notion of equality itself has undergone change over time, and a new class of rich is emerging that is rooted in the power and influence within the Communist Party. In short, inequality persists in the Soviet Union, but its form has changed.

While reviewing the manuscript for the speech, I came across a piece of news relating to the absence of equality in Russia. I reproduce it below because it throws light on the subject and lends support to my assessment. It was reported by the Canberra correspondent of 'The Sun', a well-known Australian newspaper, that the Australian Ambassador to Russia gave a statement before a parliamentary party during his holidays in which he stated:

1. A new class of wealthy people is emerging in Russia because the influential members of the Communist Party as well as those considered technical experts get far better treatment than ordinary people.
2. In restaurants the food served is graded into five classes, tickets for which can be obtained according to party influence or the nature of a person's job.
3. In consequence, the difference among individuals is as evident today as it was during Czarist Russia.
4. While in other countries the black market is run by the shadier segments of society, in Russia it is in the hands of the authorities themselves.
5. As a consequence, important people can obtain whatever they wish, while the ordinary labourer has to do without many necessities of life.

The Australian Ambassador subsequently expressed regret at the publication of the report on the ground that it was likely to upset Australia's relations with Soviet Russia. However, he did not contradict it. This suggests that the expression of regret was politically motivated and was not a contradiction of the statement itself.

This report also confirms my expectations regarding the future of Russia, as described earlier. It was inevitable that a new class of wealthy people would emerge in Russia, for the differences in individuals' capacity and calibre cannot be ignored. Because Communism lacks the restraints on power, privilege and wealth—as ordained in Islam—the new class is bound to drag Communist governments to the old ways. The only consequence of the Communist Revolution would be to give Russia a prominent place among imperialist nations in exploiting the profitable opportunities wherever available. The hope of a proletarian world government would turn into an unrealisable dream. This is so because Communist philosophy was not anchored in human sympathy, but in the goal of settling scores with the Czarist government.

Unanswered Questions About Claims of Equality

I would like to say something here about the moral and cultural standard of the ordinary Russian soldiers. I learned of the case of a train carrying drums of benzene oil through Iran. When one of the drums leaked, some Russian soldiers mistook it for rum or beer, and started drinking it. About one thousand Russian soldiers ended up drinking benzene, which resulted in the death of dozens of soldiers while hundreds were taken ill. It was a display of total lack of commitment to national service; the soldiers forgot their sense of duty and responsibility to protecting their country's property, i.e. the benzene. It also shows that the soldiers assigned in Iran were not paid enough to resist temptation and they had not benefited from Russia's economic progress.

With respect to Russian industry, the question arises whether the nature of work is similar in every industry. Clearly, a coal miner's work is quite different from that of a shopkeeper. Similarly, a tailor's needs for capital are different from the needs of a man who wants to start working as a jeweller. How does Communism propose to resolve these differences? Does the government own all the capital of the shopkeepers and control all their transactions? Further, is an incompetent doctor or a lawyer entitled to charge the same fees as other doctors and lawyers? If the fees can vary according to ability, how can the presumed claim of equality be established? And if the best doctor or a lawyer cannot charge a higher fee, would everyone not rush to them for service? In this case, how can they attend to everyone?

In short, as soon as the Communist principle of equality is put into practice, a host of questions arise. We are not in a position to know how these questions may be answered in Russia. But so long as satisfactory answers are not forthcoming, the conclusion must remain that the Communist proponents of equality are wrong in their claims.

A Proper Economic System

After reflecting over these important matters, a reasonable person would conclude that a practical economic system must leave room for religion. Short term economic considerations must not permit that the longer term consequence of an economic system be ignored. Only that economic system would be beneficial to humanity which fulfils everyone's basic needs, but also promotes healthy competition among individuals while curbing unhealthy rivalry.

The fact is that Communism was a reaction to past tyranny. That explains why this philosophy spread to areas where people were oppressed, but it did not take root in such countries as Great Britain and the United States. Similarly, it has not been successful in countries where nationalist or socialist governments were in power.

Some time ago an American newspaper posed an interesting question to the working classes: Do you consider yourself to belong to the Capitalist Class, the Middle Class or the poor class? The majority of the respondents said that they considered themselves to be in the Middle Class. This suggests that it does not occur to an American worker that he is poor. This is the reason why Communism was an even bigger failure in the United States than in Great Britain. On account of the abundance of wealth in America the labouring class does not feels that they are impoverished and are in need of a system that redresses their complaints and meets their basic needs.

Thus, the real solution to the problem is that:

1. In accordance with the Islamic teaching, the rights of the poor should be safeguarded; and
2. The hopes and aspirations of people should be fostered.

In Germany and Italy, people were not distributed money, but their aspirations were nurtured. As a consequence, they started viewing themselves as victorious and triumphant. Hope and aspirations are vital for national progress. A nation, where people no longer have aspirations or where its poor are denied basic rights, is inevitably destined to its ruin.

Responsibilities of Rich Towards Poor

The wealthy people in our country should realise their responsibilities before it is too late and should hasten to discharge the obligations they owe to poorer people. As I look at it, the emergence of Communism is a punishment against the tyrannies perpetrated by the rich upon the poor.

There is still time for improvement and to atone for excesses of the past. If wealthier people are unwilling to discharge their duties towards their less fortunate brethren, the hand of God Almighty will snatch away their wealth through this instrument [of Communism]. Repentance and appropriate action now can save you from this terrible danger and the awful storm gathering over your heads will move away to leave you in safety just as a tornado suddenly changes its course. You can either voluntarily part with a portion of your wealth for the uplift of the poor, as called upon by God; or you can face God's displeasure and continue to hold on to your wealth, which a little while later will be taken away by rebels and troublemakers.

And finally, while discussing the rise of Communism and the problems of the Russian economy, I wish to draw attention to a striking prophecy in regard to Russia made at the time when the world knew little about that area.

Prophecies About Russia

A Prophecy of More than Two Thousand Years Ago

Russia, as we know, has only come into prominence during the last three or four hundred years. Before that it was a very sparsely populated territory, whose people were split into various tribes, holding small strips of land. Even in areas that bordered on the regions now known as Russia, this endless expanse of territory had no economic or political significance. A thousand years ago, it was scarcely known, sparsely populated, and attracted little interest. Farther back in history, 2500 years ago, hardly anyone knew of it. An isolated geographer here and there might have had some vague notion of its existence, but no more. At that time Prophet Ezekiel made a striking prophecy, which is preserved in the books of the Old Testament.

EZEKIEL CHAPTER 38

1. And the word of the Lord came unto me saying.
2. Son of man, set thy face against Gog, the land of Magog, the chief prince of Meshech and prophesy against him.
3. And say, Thus saith the Lord God; Behold, I am against thee, O Gog the chief prince of Meshech and Tubal;
4. And I will turn thee back, and put hooks into thy jaws, and I will bring thee forth, and all thine army, horses and horsemen, all of them clothed with all sorts of armour even a great company with bucklers and shields, all of them handling swords.
5. Persia, Ethiopia and Libya with them; all of them with shield and helmet;
6. Gomer and all his bands; the house of Togarmah of the north quarters, and all his bands; and many people with thee.
7. Be thou prepared, and prepare for thyself, thou, and all thy company that are assembled unto thee, and be thou a guard unto them.
8. After many days thou shalt be visited; in the latter years thou shalt come into the land that is brought back from the sword, and is gathered out of many people against the mountains of Israel; which have been always waste; but it is brought forth out of the nations, and they shall dwell safely all of them.
9. Thou shalt ascend and come like a storm thou shalt be like a cloud to cover the land, thou and all thy bands, and many people with thee.

10. Thus saith the Lord God; it shall also come to pass that at the same time shall things come, into thy mind, and thou shalt think an evil thought.
11. And thou shalt say, I will go up to the land of unwalled villages; I will go to them that are at rest, that dwell safely, all of them dwelling without walls, and having neither bars nor gates.
12. To take a spoil, and to take a prey; to turn thine hand upon the desolate places that are now inhabited, and upon the people that are gathered out of the nations, which have gotten cattle and goods, that dwell in the midst of the land.
13. Sheba, and Dedan, and the merchants of Tarshish, with all the young lions thereof, shall say unto thee, Art thou come to take a spoil? hast thou gathered thy company to take a prey? To carry away silver and gold, to take away cattle and goods, to take a great spoil?
14. Therefore, son of man, prophesy and say unto Gog, Thus saith the Lord God; In that day when my people of Israel dwelleth safely, shalt thou not know it?
15. And thou shalt come from thy place out of the north parts, thou, and many people with thee, all of them riding upon horses a great company and a mighty army.
16. And thou shalt come up against my people of Israel as a cloud to cover the land; it shall be in the latter days; and I will bring thee against my land, that the heathen may know me, when I shall be sanctified in thee, O Gog, before their eyes.
17. Thus saith the Lord God; Art thou he of whom I have spoken in old time by my servants the prophets of Israel

which prophesied in those days many years that I would bring thee against them?

18. And it shall come to pass at the same time when Gog shall come against the land of Israel, saith the Lord God, that my fury shall come up in my face.

19. For in my jealousy and in the fire of my wrath have I spoken Surely in that day there shall be a great shaking in the land of Israel;

20. So that the fishes of the sea, and the fowls of the heaven, and the beasts of the field and all creeping things that creep upon the earth and all the men that are upon the face of the earth, shall shake at my presence and the mountains shall be thrown down, and the steep places shall fall, and every wall shall fall to the ground.

21. And I will call for a sword against him throughout all my mountains saith the Lord God every man's sword shall be against his brother.

22. And I will plead against him with pestilence and with blood; and I will rain upon him and upon his bands and upon the many people that are with him, an overflowing rain, and great hailstones, fire, and brimstone.

23. Thus will I magnify myself, and sanctify myself; and I will be known in the eyes of many nations, and they shall know that I *am* the LORD.

EZEKIEL CHAPTER 39

1. Therefore, thou son of man prophesy against Gog and say, Thus saith the Lord God; Behold, I am against thee, O Gog, the chief prince of Meshech and Tubal.
2. And I will turn thee back and leave but the sixth part of thee and will cause thee to come up from the north parts, and will bring thee upon the mountains of Israel.
3. And I will smite thy bow out of thy left hand, and will cause thine arrows to fall out of thy right hand.
4. Thou shalt fall upon the mountains of Israel thou, and all thy bands, and the people that is with thee: I will give thee unto the ravenous birds of every sort and to the beasts of the field to be devoured.
5. Thou shalt fall upon the open field: for I have spoken it, saith the Lord God.
6. And I will send a fire on Magog, and among them that dwell carelessly in the isles; and they shall know that I am the Lord.
7. So will I make my holy name known in the midst of my people Israel; and I will not let them pollute my holy name any more and the heathen shall know that I am the Lord, the Holy One in Israel.
8. Behold, it is come, and it is done saith the Lord God; this is the day whereof I have spoken.
9. And they that dwell in the cities of Israel shall go forth and shall set on fire and burn the weapons both the shields and the bucklers, the bows and the arrows and the handstaves

and the spears and they shall burn them with fire seven years.
10. So that they shall take no wood cut out of the field, neither cut down any out of the forests, for they shall burn the weapons with fire; and they shall spoil those that spoiled them, and rob those that robbed them, saith the Lord God.
11. And it shall come to pass in that day, that I will give unto Gog a place there of graves in Israel, the valley of the passengers on the east of the sea: and it shall stop the noses of the passengers: and there shall they bury Gog and all his multitude: and they shall call it The valley of Ha-mon-gog.
12. And seven months shall the house of Israel be burying of them, that they may cleanse the land.
13. Yea, all the people of the land shall bury them; and it shall be to them a renown the day that I shall be glorified saith the Lord God.
14. And they shall sever out men of continual employment passing through the land to bury with the passengers those that remain upon the face of the earth, to cleanse it; after the end of seven months shall they search.
15. And the passengers that pass through the land, when any seeth a man's bone, then shall he set up a sign by it, till the buriers have buried it in the valley of Ha-mon-Gog.
16. And also the name of the city shall be Hamonah. Thus shall they cleanse the land;
17. And, thou son of man, thus saith the Lord God; speak unto every feathered fowl, and to every beast of the field. Assemble yourselves, and come; gather yourselves on every side to my sacrifice that I do sacrifice for you even a great

sacrifice upon the mountains of Israel that ye may eat flesh, and drink blood.
18. Ye shall eat the flesh of the mighty and drink the blood of the princes of the earth, of rams, of lambs, and of goats, of bullocks, all of them fatlings of Bashan.
19. And ye shall eat fat till ye be full and drink blood till ye be drunken, of my sacrifice which I have sacrificed for you.
20. Thus ye shall be filled at my table with horses and chariots, with mighty men, and with all men of war, saith the Lord God.
21. And I will set my glory among the heathen, and all the heathen shall see my judgement that I have executed, and my hand that I have laid upon them.

Made at a time when Russia was entirely unknown to the outside world, and when nobody could imagine that it would attain such progress and domination, this prophecy is remarkably clear. It tells us that:

'Meshech and Tubal (Moscow and Russia) will attain great power and glory until, aware of their strength, they would try to subjugate other countries and snatch away their wealth.' We should note that according to the words of this prophesy, Persia would one day be reduced to submission by Moscow. (The foundations for which are being laid in the current Russian demand for oil concessions from Iran.)

...'Carry away silver and gold, to take away cattle and goods, to take a great spoil' (This portion of the prophecy indicates that Russian imperialism would be even more dangerous for the other countries than the earlier forms of imperialism.) We are told that

Russia would leap forward in wave after wave of unchecked conquests until it would begin to dream of holding sway over Jerusalem, lying defenceless in the path of its victorious hordes. Then God's wrath would be kindled and a rain of fire and sulphur would descend upon it, and its jaws would be broken by heavy piercing blows which would bring such utter destruction that its dead would lie in heaps in the valleys and it would take months to cover them up with earth.

To people who do not believe in prophesies, I would like to say that if there was no God who gave His Apostles fore-knowledge of mighty events, then who was it that told Ezekiel two thousand and five hundred years ago that Russia would embark upon a program of world conquest, aggression and aggrandisement, so that God's wrath would be kindled against it and the punishment from heaven would leave its power in ruins. When we give due thought to this prophecy and the extraordinary manner in which it has come true in our own days, we are forced to conclude that God who conveys such tidings to His chosen servants really does exist. And if God does exist, and He gave to Ezekiel fore-knowledge of these events, we must also bear in mind that God Almighty does not wish that the Communist system, which forms the basis of Russia's political economy and social structure, should be permanently established in the world; and that its downfall is not very far away.

Prophecy of the Promised Messiah^{as} Regarding Russia

Now let me turn to a prophecy about Russia that God revealed to the Founder of the Ahmadiyya Movement, informing him that Russia's Czar was about to face a very serious calamity:

زار بھی ہوگا تو ہوگا اُس گھڑی با حالِ زار

(*Barāhīn-e-Aḥmadiyyah*, part 5, *Rūḥānī Khazā'in*, vol. 21, p. 152)

That is: The day is coming when the Czar of Russia would be reduced to a very miserable plight. As we all know, the reigning Czar and his family were captured and killed after the Red Revolution after suffering untold privations and humiliations. It is one of the most painful and tragic episodes of human history.

Another prophecy made by the Promised Messiah[as] in regard to Russia was recorded by him as follows:[26]

> On January 22, 1903, I saw in a vision that the sceptre of the Czar of Russia had come into my hand. It was very long and beautiful. But examining it carefully I found that it was a gun, though it had not the appearance of one. It had secret barrels and outwardly appeared to be no more than a sceptre, while it was also really a gun. (*al-Ḥakam*, no. 4, vol. 7, January 31, 1903, p. 15:3)

---

[26] In *Tadhkirah* second English edition a reference to this vision/dream appears on p. 591 with some variation of words, under the date January 30, 1903. (publishers)

Being given the sceptre of a country, in a revelatory vision, signifies that the recipient will be granted power and influence over that country. Thus Prophet Ezekiel's prophecy informs us that God is not in favour of the establishment of the Communist rule, and if the new rulers do not seek God's forgiveness, but continue to interfere in the internal affairs of other nations, they will face God's wrath and severe punishment. But the Promised Messiah[as] has given us the glad tiding that the direction and control of Russia's affairs would one day pass into the hands of Ahmadis who would be assigned the responsibility of reforming the system.

These prophecies from God Almighty were made at a time when there were few indications of their being fulfilled, and this is so even today. I place these prophecies before the thousands of people gathered here today to listen to my address.

The words of the Prophet Ezekiel were given to the world six hundred years before Christ; in other words, more than two thousand and five hundred years ago. At that time, very little was known of Russia, and it was unimaginable that it would assume such power and influence over other countries. The more we think, the more we are struck by the grandeur of the prophecy.

Then there is the prophecy of the Promised Messiah[as] regarding the extinction of Czar's reign, whose fulfilment has been witnessed by the whole world. The Promised Messiah's second prophecy foresees the collapse of the Soviet rule and the handover of its guiding control into the hands of the Promised Messiah[as].

The Holy Prophet Muhammad[sa] was shown in a vision that the keys of the treasuries of the Roman and Persian Empires had been put into his hands, but they actually came into the hands of his followers, during the days of Ḥaḍrat Umar[ra], In a similar way, the sceptre of Russia would one day pass, according to this prophecy, into the hands of the Promised Messiah's followers. Prophecies made by God's Prophets are not necessarily fulfilled in their own time, but later as the history of religions shows, at the hands of their followers.

It is not a fanciful dream but our conviction that God has put us in charge of removing Russia's evils and reforming the Soviet system and that one day the Russian people will embrace Ahmadiyyat and establish the system we have described. Sooner or later, the danger that Communism poses will disappear and the world will come to realise that the only remedy for the world's ills and afflictions lies in adopting the Islamic teachings.

A Dream Bearing upon Destruction of Communism

Twenty-four years ago I saw in a dream that I was standing in the middle of a vast plain and a monster in the form of a huge serpent was approaching in the distance. Its proportions might have been as much as twenty yards in length and a thickness of the trunk of a giant tree. As the monster approached, it seemed that it had started from one end of the earth, devouring everything along the way. When it reached the point where I was standing, it turned towards an Ahmadi, who started to run to escape the reptile. At that moment, I grabbed a big staff and started to chase the monster in order to rescue the Ahmadi. But I found that the monster was running so fast that I had no chance of overtaking it. All the same, I continued to run, and then I saw that the Ahmadi had reached a tree, which he started to climb in haste. But before he could climb high enough, the reptile reached him and swallowed the Ahmadi in a single mouthful. Then the monster turned in anger at me for having tried to rescue its prey. But as it ran to attack me I saw the frame of a *charpai* (Indian bedstead) lying close to where I stood. As soon as the serpent came close, I jumped on to this frame and managed to stand astride on its two opposite bars. As the reptile came closer, I heard some people asking me how I could hope to fight it when the Holy Prophet[sa] had said that there was no one who could subdue it.

I realised then that this monster was none other than the Gog and Magog to whom this hadith referred and that the monster was in fact the *dajjāl*. At that point, I raised both hands towards heaven in prayer for God's help and protection. Responding to the Ahmadis by my side who had pointed out to me the futility trying to fight the monster, I said that I did not seek to fight it through my own powers, but through the power of prayer; and that victory by this means was not precluded by what the Holy Prophet[sa] had said. As I prayed, I noticed a change was coming over the serpent, just like little mountain insects that start to melt when salt is poured over them. I noticed that it had started to lose its fire and speed, until it became completely dormant. It then assumed a jelly-like form, which melted into watery liquid that began to flow away. I turned to my companions and said, 'Did you observe the power of prayer? Of course, I did not have the strength to overcome the danger I faced, but my God certainly had the power to remove it'.

Concluding Observations

It must be kept in mind that we, the Ahmadis, bear enmity to no one; we desire the good and well-being of all. Even for our worst enemies we do not bear the slightest feeling of ill will. All we wish to see is that good character prevails in the world, man's spiritual life progresses, and the Kingdom of God and His Apostle gets established. We desire that whatever social, economic, cultural or political system is adopted in the world, it should leave to God and His Apostle the sphere of human life that rightfully and properly belongs to them; that people who wish to live by God's laws should not be made to deny them.

We bear no enmity against Russia, or Communism. I personally harbour deep sympathy for this great country, and sincerely wish that the Russian people, who have been victims of extreme cruelty for centuries, should march forward and witness prosperous times. But I or any other freedom-loving person cannot bear to watch that a misconceived social order and political philosophy become an instrument of subjugating other people. As such, we would look upon any system that incorporated in itself the Islamic principles in regard to these matters as our own and shall endeavour to support it to the best of our ability. Otherwise, we are duty bound to oppose systems that seek to push religion out of its proper sphere in the life of human beings. Hunger, no doubt, involves terrible suffering for those who have to bear its pangs; but we are not prepared to sacrifice our religion even for the sake of keeping off hunger and want from our hearths and homes.

In my presentation this afternoon, I have greatly compressed the subject and have left out many things. But even so, I have taken a good deal of your time. Now that I have brought out the contrast between essential economic principles as visualised by Islam, on one side, and Communism, on the other, I trust that you will consider these issue more thoroughly and will not get carried away by mere hearsay or slogans. Intellectual progress requires that before adopting any course of action, careful and critical consideration be given to all aspects of an issue. Thus, in adopting any path or system, we must use our minds and have our eyes open. And it is essential that whatever views we adopt we should adopt after the most careful scrutiny; whatever course we follow, we should follow it with our eyes open. This is the only way that one can find truth and bring an end to unrest and disorder.

May Allah have mercy on me and enable me to follow the path of His guidance and pleasure. May He give to you as well the wisdom and strength to follow the path full of blessings for you and for your generations to come both in your spiritual and religious life as well as your secular life. I conclude with: *All praise belongs to Allah, Lord of all the worlds.*

PUBLISHERS' NOTE

Please note that according to our system of counting Quranic verses, the verse *Bismillāhir-Raḥmānir-Raḥīm* (In the name of Allah, the Most Gracious, Ever Merciful) is counted as the first verse of the chapter which it precedes. Some publishers of the Holy Quran, however, begin counting following *Bismillāhir-Raḥmānir-Raḥīm*. Should the reader not find the relevant verse under the number mentioned in this book, he or she is advised to deduct 1 from the number. For example, if this book quotes Ch. 35: *Fāṭir:* 25, then some copies of the Holy Quran will list the same verse under Ch. 35: *Fāṭir:* 24.

Where necessary, translation of the Arabic text has been elaborated by additional words to explain the meaning. Such words are in italics. The word *and* at the commencement of a translated verse has been omitted.

The form *ibn* has been used in both initial and medial position in the names of persons, in order to conform to current usage, although *bin* also occurs medially in some original texts (abbreviated usually as *b*).

Quotations from the Holy Bible are from King James version.

The name of Muhammad[sa], the Holy Prophet of Islam, has been followed by the symbol [sa], which is an abbreviation of (ﷺ)

Ṣallallāhu 'Alaihi Wa Ālihī Wasallam (may peace and blessings of Allah be upon him and his progeny). The names of other Prophets[as] are followed by the symbol [as], an abbreviation of (عليه السلام/عليهم السلام) 'Alaihissalām/'Alaihimussalām (on whom be peace). The actual prayers have not generally been set out in full, but they should nevertheless, be understood as being repeated in full in each case. The symbol [ra] is used with the name of the Companions of the Holy Prophet[sa] and those of the Promised Messiah[as]. It is an abbreviation of (رضي الله عنه/عنها/عنهم) Raḍiyallāhu 'anhu/'anhā/'anhum (may Allah be pleased with him/with her/with them). We have used [rh] for (رحمه الله) Raḥimahullāhu Ta'ālā (may Allah's blessing be on him). Finally, [aa] stands for (أيده الله) Ayyadahullāhu Ta'ālā (may Allah, the Almighty help him).

In transliterating Arabic words we have followed the following system adopted by the Royal Asiatic Society:

- ا   at the beginning of a word, pronounced as *a, i, u* preceded by a very slight aspiration, like *h* in the English word *honour*.
- ث   *th*, pronounced like *th* in the English word *thing*.
- ح   *ḥ*, a guttural aspirate, stronger than *h*.
- خ   *kh*, pronounced like the Scotch *ch* in *loch*.
- ذ   *dh*, pronounced like the English *th* in *that*.
- ص   *ṣ*, strongly articulated *s*.
- ض   *ḍ*, similar to the English *th* in *this*.
- ط   *ṭ*, strongly articulated palatal *t*.
- ظ   *ẓ*, strongly articulated *z*.
- ع   ʻ, a strong guttural, the pronunciation of which must be learnt by the ear.

غ   *gh*, a sound approached very nearly in the *r grasseye* in French, and in the German *r*. It requires the muscles of the throat to be in the 'gargling' position whilst pronouncing it.

ق   *q*, a deep guttural *k* sound.

ئ   ', a sort of catch in the voice.

Short vowels are represented by:
- *a* for ◌َ (like *u* in *bud*)
- *i* for ◌ِ (like *i* in *bid*)
- *u* for ◌ُ (like *oo* in *wood*)

Long vowels by:
- *ā* for ◌ا or آ (like *a* in *father*);
- *ī* for ى ◌ِ or ◌ِي (like *ee* in *deep*);
- *ū* for و ◌ُ (like *oo* in *root*);

Other:
- *ai* for ى ◌َ (like *i* in *site*);[27]
- *au* for و ◌َ (resembling *ou* in *sound*)

Please note that in transliterated words the letter *e* is to be pronounced as in *prey* which rhymes with *day*; however the pronunciation is flat without the element of English diphthong. If in Urdu and Persian words *e* is lengthened a bit more, it is transliterated as *ei* to be pronounced as *ei* in *feign* without the element of diphthong.

---

[27] In Arabic words like شيخ (Shaikh) there is an element of diphthong which is missing when the word is pronounced in Urdu. (publishers)

Thus ک is transliterated as *kei*. For the nasal sound of *n* we have used the symbol *ń*. Thus the Urdu word میں is transliterated as *meiń*.[28]

The consonants not included in the above list have the same phonetic value as in the principal languages of Europe.

We have not transliterated foreign words which have become part of English language, e.g., Islam, Mahdi, Quran,[29] Hijra, Ramadan, hadith, ulama, umma, sunna, kafir, pukka, etc.

Curved commas are used in the system of transliteration, ' for ع, ' for ء. Commas as punctuation marks are used according to the normal usage. Similarly, normal usage is followed for the apostrophe.

We have made every effort to validate the original references and have also added several additional references where needed.

The Royal Asiatic Society rules of transliteration for names of persons, places and other terms, could not be followed throughout the book as many of the names contain non-Arabic characters and carry a local transliteration and pronunciation style which in itself is also not consistent either.

---

[28] These transliterations are not included in the system of transliteration by The Royal Asiatic Society. (publishers)

[29] Concise Oxford Dictionary records Quran in three forms—Quran, Qur'an and Koran. (publishers)

GLOSSARY

Ahmadiyya Muslim Jamāʿat—The Community of Muslims who have accepted the claims of Ḥaḍrat Mirza Ghulam Ahmad[as] of Qadian as the Promised Messiah and Mahdi. The Community was established by Ḥaḍrat Mirza Ghulam Ahmad[as] in 1889, and is now under the leadership of his fifth *Khalīfah*—Ḥaḍrat Mirza Masroor Ahmad (may Allah be his help). The Community is also known as Jamāʿat-e-Ahmadiyya. A member of the Community is called an Ahmadi Muslim or simply an Ahmadi.

Alḥamdulillāh—A phrase from the Holy Quran meaning, all praise belongs to Allah alone.

Allah—Allah is the personal name of God in Islam. To show proper reverence to Him, Muslims often add *Taʿālā*, translated here as 'the Exalted', when saying His Holy name.

Anjuman—An administrative body established by the Promised Messiah[as] for the administration of the affairs of the Ahmadiyya Muslim Community.

Dhil-qurbā—*See page 66*

Ḥaḍrat—A term of respect used for a person of established righteousness and piety.

Hadith—A saying of the Holy Prophet Muhammad[sa]. The plural is *āḥādīth*.

Holy Prophet[sa]—A term used exclusively for the Founder of Islam, Ḥaḍrat Muhammad, may peace and blessings of Allah be upon him.

Holy Quran—The Book sent by Allah for the guidance of mankind. It was revealed word by word to the Holy Prophet Muhammad[sa] over a period of twenty-three years.

Iḥtikār—*See page 57*

Jamā'at—Jamā'at means community. Although the word *jamā'at* itself may refer to any community, in this book, Jamā'at specifically refers to the Ahmadiyya Muslim Jamā'at.

Khalīfah and Khilāfat—Caliph is derived from the Arabic word *Khalīfah*, which herein means the successor. *Khulafā'* is the plural of *Khalīfah*. In Islamic terminology, the title *'Khalīfa-e-Rāshid'* [righteous *Khalīfah*] is applied to one of the first four *khulafā'* who continued the mission of the Holy Prophet Muhammad[sa]. Ahmadi Muslims refer to each successor of the Promised Messiah[as] as Khalīfatul-Masīḥ. The institution of successorship is called *Khilāfat*.

Khalīfatul-Masīḥ II—Ḥaḍrat Khalīfatul-Masīḥ II, Mirza Bashir-ud-Din Mahmud Ahmad[ra] (1889–1965), was the second successor of the Promised Messiah[as]. He is also called Muṣleḥ-e-Mauʿūd because he was born in accordance with the prophecy made by the Promised Messiah[as] in 1886 concerning the birth of a righteous son who would be endowed with unique abilities and attributes.

Khalīfatul-Masīḥ V—Ḥaḍrat Khalīfatul-Masīḥ V, Mirza Masroor Ahmad[aa], is the fifth successor of the Promised Messiah[as] and the current Imam of Jamāʿat-e-Ahmadiyya. He is the great grandson of the Promised Messiah[as].

Khilāfat—The institution of successorship in Islam. *See also* **Khalīfah.**

Khumus—*See page* 61

Laghw— *See page* 45

Lubad—*See page* 23

Mahdi—'The guided one.' This is the title given by the Holy Prophet Muhammad[sa] to the awaited Reformer of the Latter Days.

Muhammad[sa]—Proper name of the Holy Prophet[sa] of Islam.

Ribā—*See under heading* Barriers to Illegitimate Accumulation of Wealth in Islam: Prohibition of Interest (Riba) *on page 53*

Qaḍā—*See page* 80

Taṣawwuf—*See page* 80

The Promised Messiah—This term refers to the Founder of the Ahmadiyya Muslim Jamāʿat, Ḥaḍrat Mirza Ghulam Ahmad[as] of Qadian. He claimed that he had been sent by Allah in accordance with the prophecies of the Holy Prophet[sa] about the coming of *al-Imam al-Mahdi* (the Guided Leader) and Messiah.

Sūrah—A term in Arabic referring to a chapter of the Holy Quran.

Zakat—*See page* 60

INDEX

Accountability
    to God for discharging
        the trust, 3
Antique
    wasteful expenditure on, 46
Appropriate Economic System
    must make room for religion, 124
Asant's revolt in Russia
    reasons of, 92
Autarchy
    cannot continue indefinitely in Russia, 107
Authority
    Islamic injunctions to those in, 5
    must be exercised within prescribed limits, 5
Bank loans
    leveraging, as an instrument of amassing wealth, 53

Cartels
    unlawfulness of, 56
Communism
    considers religious work to be useless activity., 76
    deprives an individual to work for the life Hereafter, 74
    destroys filial love, 102
    divine punishment against oppression, 125
    does not prohibit interest, 98
    fails on the criterion of reason and common sense, 85
    failure to implement its ideals about land holding, 91
    false in claiming no concern with religion, 77
    force needed to uphold, 96

injustice to farmers
under, 91
interference in the rights
of property., 87
objections against, on the
basis of religion, 74
practical ban on religious
studies under, 78
requires compulsion, 101
similarity with Islam on
meeting the primary
needs, 72
three major claims of, 72
Communist(s)
leaves no margin for
voluntary religious
work, 76
not prepared to tolerate
any religion, 84
Compulsion
needed to run the
Communist ideas, 101
Currency manipulation
by Germany and Russia
after World War I,
100
Dedication of life
importance of, in Islam,
79
Desire to accumulate wealth
incentives for, 40
Dhil-qurbā
defined, 66

Domestic obligations
become acts of charity if
done for the sake of
God's pleasure, 38
Economic competition
and selfishness, 40
Economic equality
unanswered questions
about, 123
Economic philosophy of
Islam
can only succeed in an
environment of
Islamic teachings, 17
Economic system of Islam
foundation of, 1
importance of the subject,
1
two fundamental
principles of, 36
Economic Systems
three types of, 15
Economics
and slavery, 35
Egalitarian society
by curbing the incentives
to earn illicit wealth,
47
Elections
real criterion for, 10
Equality
cannot be achieved
completely, 85

Equality in Russia
  doubts about, 120
Equitable distribution of
    wealth
  ban on interest needed
    for, 54
Excessive wealth
  Islam reject the motives
    leading to, 52
Extravagance
  Islam forbids, 48
Filial bonds
  strength of, 103
Filial Love
  destroyed by
    Communism, 102
Fiqah
  defined, 80
Germany
  migration of Jews out of,
    104
Gibbon
  on the prayer of Malek
    Shah, 11
Governance
  four basic precepts about,
    9
Hadrat Abu Bakr[ra]
  selfless services for
    Islam, 13
Hadrat Adam[as]
  earliest revelations relate
    to meeting the
    primary needs, 69

his paradise was no
  earth, not in the
  heavens, 70
Hadrat Umar[ra]
  census initiated by, 68
  enlightened view of
    slavery, 30
  example of market
    regulation by, 58
  Martyrdom of, 33
  night watches of, 68
Harth
  meaning of, 6
Hereafter.
  belief in, entails the belief
    in freedom of choice,
    36
Hoarding of wealth
  rejected by Islam, 51
Holy Quran
  authority is a trust, 12
Idle gossip
  as an example of what is
    laghw, 45
Ihtikār
  defined, 57
Imperialism
  shifting of Russia
    towards, as foreign
    trade grows, 105
Individual freedom
  a key component of
    Islamic economic
    system, 39

an essential requirement
of Islamic philosophy,
37
needed to provide
incentives and
healthy competition,
39
Individual initiative
promoted by Islam,
curbed by
Communism, 73
Individualistic economic
system
defined, 16
Inheritance
and redistribution of land
under Islamic law, 88
Intellectual Excellence
not recognized in
Communism, 103
Interest
not rejected in the
Communist
philosophy, 97
Interest (ribā)
as an instrument of
economic control, 53
defined, 54
prohibition of, 53
Islam
redistributes wealth by
persuation, not
compulsion, 101
Islam's Economic Philosophy
foundation of, 17

Islamic economic system
compared to a well-
planned orchard, 16
four basic features of, 71
fundamental same as
those of Islam itself, 17
Islamic Economic System
essence of, 39
Islamic history
slavery never used as an
instrument of
economic
development, 31
Islamic system
operation of, in land
ownership, 90
Jewellery
allowed for women within
limits, 46
Karl Marx
writings on Communism
derive their origin in
the industrial setting,
87
Khumus
defined, 61
Kingdoms
a trust from God, 3
Kingship
no room for hereditor,
in Islam, 10
Laghw
defined, 45
Islam does not approve
of, 45

Land holdings
  Islamic scheme to reduce, 91
Land ownership
  operation of Islamic law in, 90
Law of Inheritance
  as a potent way of distributing wealth, 61
Laws of inheritance
  wisdom of, 88
Lubad
  defined, 23
Malek Shah
  Noble prayer of, 11
Mankind
  everything in the world created for the benefit of, 17
Markets
  need to find new, with industrial expansion, 108
  supplies should not be withheld from, 56
Marshal Malinovsky
  and concept of work in Communism, 83
Monopoly
  example of the tactics of, 55
National Progress
  uplifting of poor necessary for, 21

Nizamud-Din Toosi, 11
Oilfields of Iran
  Russia's eyes upon, 116
Orphans
  exhortations for sympathy for, 25
Ownership of wealth
  belongs to God, 20
  Ḥaḍrat Shuʿaib on, 19
Poverty
  description of extreme, 25
Price fixation
  dangers of, 58
Primary needs
  Islamic state obligated to meet, for all, 67
Prisoners of war
  freedom by paying ransom, 31
  injunction to help in procuring their freedom, 18
  teachings of Islam about freeing, 31
Prisoners of War
  permitted only in a regular, declared war, 29
Private gardens
  as an example of extravagance, 48
Prophet Ezekiel
  prophecy of, about Russia, 126

Qaḍā
  defined, 80
Regulation of markets
  an idea introduced by
    Islam, 57
Religious education
  obstructed in
    Communism under
    the excuse of freedom
    of choice, 84
Ribā. See Interest (ribā)
Rich
  Islam's admonitions to, 26
  responsibilities towards
    the poor, 125
Rights of Property
  Communism interferes
    with, 87
Russia
  economic growth between
    1928 and 1937 in, 106
  occupation of
    neighbouring
    countries by, 111
Russian industry
  danger of decline in, 104
  inevitability of facing
    international
    competition, 105
Russian Occupied Territories
  absence of equality in, 110
Shariah
  instructs rulers to act with
    justice, 9
  ordains that rulers be
    appointed through
    elections, 8
Sir William Muir, 27
  views about the earliest
    four Sūrahs, 22
Slavery
  and economic
    development, 28
  and economics, 35
  as source of cheap labour,
    29
  Islam leaves no room for
    any person to enslave
    another, 32
  main motive for
    practicing was
    economic
    development, 29
  stopping of, by Islam, 28
Slaves
  Two methods of
    acquiring in past, 28
Sources of wealth
  Islamic concept of, 17
Sovereignty
  belongs to God alone, 2
Soviet Russia.
  ill treatment of an
    Ahmadi Missionary
    in, 75
Spiritual merit
  depends upon virtuous
    acts performed
    voluntarily, 36

State Capitalism
  danger of, 114
State intervention
  a key component of
    Islamic economic
    system, 39
  needed to safeguard the
    weaker sections of
    society, 39
Stephen King-Hall
  aims of Russian
    Communism, 93
Supply and demand
  free interplay of, 58
Sympathy for the poor
  ordained in the earliest
    revelations in Islam,
    21
Tafsīr
  an important branch of
    learning, 80
Taj Mahal
  not money well spent, 49
  technical, engineering,
    and artistic beauty of,
    49
Taṣawwuf
  defined, 80
Teachings of Islam
  most comprehansive of all
    religions, 79
Trusts
  unlawulness of, 54
Uphill ascent
  concept of, in the Holy
    Quran, 25
Use of Wealth
  Islam's verdict on, 18
Voluntary charity
  prescribed for the care of
    orphans and poor, 61
Voluntary sacrifices
  as seeds to be harvested
    for the Hereafter, 37
Volunteer work
  for those who do not need
    to work for a living,
    45
Wealth
  redistribution through
    the laws of
    inheritance, 62
Zakat
  defined, 60